DEMS

Demos is an independent think tank committed to radical think-ing on the long-term problems facing the UK and other advanced industrial societies.

It aims to develop ideas – both theoretical and practical – to help shape the politics of the twenty first century, and to improve the breadth and quality of political debate.

Demos publishes books and a regular journal and undertakes substantial empirical and policy oriented research projects. Demos is a registered charity.

In all its work Demos brings together people from a wide range of backgrounds in business, academia, government, the volun-tary sector and the media to share and cross-fertilise ideas and experiences.

For further information and
subscription details please contact:
Demos
9 Bridewell Place
London EC4V 6AP
Telephone: 0171 353 4479
Facsimile: 0171 353 4481
email: mail@demos.co.uk

Other publications available from Demos:

After Social Democracy
The British Spring
An end to illusions
The Future of Privacy, vols 1 and 2
Holistic Government
The Post-Modern State and the World Order
Tomorrow's Politics

To order a publication or
a free catalogue please contact
Demos (details overleaf).

On the right lines

*The next centre-right in
the British Isles*

Perri 6

DEMOS

First published in 1998 by
Demos
9 Bridewell Place
London EC4V 6AP
Telephone: 0171 353 4479
Facsimile: 0171 353 4481
email: mail@demos.co.uk
© Demos 1998

ISBN 1 898309 99 X
Printed in Great Britain by Redwood Books
Design by Lindsay Nash

Contents

About the author

Perri 6 is Director of Policy and Research at Demos. His recent publications include *The Future of Privacy* (two volumes), *Holistic Government*, *Escaping Poverty: From safety nets to networks of opportunity* (all available from Demos); *Liberty, Charity and Politics* (with A Randon, Dartmouth Publishing); and *The Contract Culture in Public Services* (edited with J Kendall, Ashgate). He is currently engaged in a major study of 'Tomorrow's Government'.

Acknowledgements

I am grateful to the many people for discussions over some months and years that have worked their way into this text, and to several people in particular for their comments on an early draft of this book: Tim Boswell, Ian Christie, Michael Gove, John Gray, Tim Hames, Ian Hargreaves, Danny Kruger, Roger Scruton, and Bob Tyrrell. It should not be imagined that any of them necessarily agrees with my argument, nor are they responsible for any errors in this text.

Introduction

When – and I mean 'when', not 'if' – the centre-right returns to be a major force in British culture, life and government, it is quite possible that it will not be conservative. Indeed, conservatism is a very particular kind of centre-right culture, tradition and movement, not found everywhere in the world, and for all its longevity in Britain, not necessarily even appropriate for all time in Britain for the centre-right.

In any viable society there springs up some kind of centre-right political practice. Whatever your personal politics, it matters very much just what kind of centre-right we might have in the twenty-first century. For, like the centre-left, the centre-right articulates certain abiding impulses without which culture, economy and society become unbalanced and run dangers of several kinds of tyranny. Any deeply rooted political culture has several deeply rooted commitments – if they had but one each, they would be single issue campaigns, not cultures at all. Inevitably, these commitments come into tension with one another. In each generation, therefore, these tensions have to be resolved in a way that balances the rival needs of desire for coherence of policy with the importance of assembling broad coalitions of support.

In the case of the centre-right, those abiding commitments are for social order, private property, both authority *and* liberty, both individualism *and* community, modernisation *and* continuity.[1] For the centre-left, we might point to basic commitments of equality, social justice, public accountability: for the radical centre, meritocracy, liberty *and* cultural commitment, transparency, competition and modernisation – perhaps even for their own sakes – *but also* for social grounding.

In addition to basic commitments, political currents also possess certain distinctive skills and capacities. The centre-right has an ability to engage in a certain messy, untidy style of institutional creativity that often proves more robust than the too tidy-minded institutional structures of the centre-left.

The challenge for the centre-right today is to develop a new settlement between its abiding commitments and to nurture afresh its skills and capacities in ways that will prepare it once again to offer a credible political direction.

After the electoral defeat of the Conservative Party in Britain in 1997, the centre-right is engaged in rethinking its role, aims, means and resources. A policy review has been announced. But what the party – and indeed the wider currents of centre-right political thought and practice in Britain and the rest of the developed world – needs first is a review of its fundamental philosophy. Until it becomes clear what the centre-right is basically for, clarity about particular policies will have neither relevance nor electoral appeal.

Unfortunately, in recent years, the centre-right in the Conservative Party in Britain has been much clearer about what it stands against than what it stands for. And this is true beyond Britain. Just as the British public has heard from Conservatives that they are against a federal European state, so for many years the Republican Party in the US appeared mainly to be against communism and big government. French Gaullists and German Christian Democrats face different but surprisingly analogous situations. Indeed, British Conservatives will undertake this rethinking not in national isolation but along side and together with the centre-right in the US, France and even Germany, where the centre-left appears for the moment to be in the ascendant.

The centre-right in the rest of the world is not in quite the same parlous state. In western Europe, centre-right parties hold power in Spain and in Norway. Ireland has two centre-right parties and one is in power at the moment. In Israel and in parts of Latin America, the centre-right is reasonably healthy. In the Czech Republic, for the first time since the fall of communism the centre-right lost overall control. Moreover, recently, the centre-right won power again in Hungary. The centre-right traditions in these countries are genuinely very different indeed – in France and Germany, the centre-right has only spasmodically been conservative in the anglophone sense of the word, since the Second World War. Christian Democracy and Gaullist republicanism draw on at least some different roots from those on which English and many recent Scots conservatives draw.[2]

Yet, despite the divergence of their roots, the centre-right in the countries where it is in trouble faces crises that are remarkably similar. There are some global and secular forces that have brought difficulties for some traditional centre-right commitments, just as in the 1970s and 1980s there were global and secular forces that rendered much of the tradition of the centre-left irrelevant and impotent.

Moreover, some of the risks that the centre-right faces in Europe and North America are alarmingly similar. Where the centre-right has been weak, divided or failed to modernise itself, there has grown up once again in Europe and in some parts of the USA a new xenophobic, racist and embittered populist far right. Only in the Scandinavian and Iberian states is the far right now largely irrelevant. In France, Germany, Austria and parts of the US, the failure of the centre-right to rethink its role has led it to compete with the far right on xenophobia or else to strike deals with far right candidates or even parties. Britain has, to date, been largely immune from this, and the British far right has been, thankfully, more often incompetent and ridiculous than a major danger. But there is nothing inevitable about this. One part of the challenge for the British centre-right now is to size the opportunity to reinvent itself in ways that will ensure the continued marginalisation of the extreme right.

In this book, I want to explore the resources that are available to the centre-right in Britain and to consider which might become of greatest relevance in its reconstruction.

Anyone who sets about such a thing ought to put their own personal political cards on the table, if only that readers whose convictions are from the centre-right know whether the writer is friend or foe. I am not a conservative. But nor am I on the centre-left, although like many people, I once was. My personal politics are of the radical centre. At the moment, many on the radical centre are allied with the centre-left. It was not always so. Indeed, during the late 1980s, many on the radical centre were in alliance with the centre-right. Such are the common contingencies of pragmatic politics, and many on the centre-right may now feel bitter about the fickleness of fair-weather friends. But the radical centre also tends to be a foul-weather friend to the politics of the currents on the centre-right and centre-left. Fearing that imbalance could allow in extremism or simply the erosion of a viable democratic and liberal political culture, it tends to be concerned that whichever strand of the democratic politics of civil society is in most urgent need of rejuvenation and reconnection should also deserve the attention of radical centrists themselves.

Moreover, people from outside any tradition or culture can sometimes offer a helpful contribution, and the aim of this book is to be helpful to the centre-right. Because I believe that the centre-right is a vital ballast in any viable political culture, I have absolutely no desire to make a case that would, if adopted, serve the centre-right ill. Nor do I wish to persuade those on the centre-right to adopt the positions of the radical centre. This book does not even describe, let alone develop or still less advocate those positions. The vital contribution that the centre-right makes to viable democratic politics is one that it makes as a coalition or settlement of strands of thought that belong genuinely to the centre-right. The contribution of the radical centre is quite different, but there is and must be a symbiosis between them.

This is not the tract of an *agent provocateur* or an infiltrator, but an attempt to be dispassionate about the best interests of a vital political culture of which I do not happen to be part, but which plays a crucial role in securing the viability of our common life. The point about the outsider's contribution, like the consultant's advice, is precisely that it may lack the fire and commitment of the partisan insider, and while it will surely miss some of the vital motivations, it may also spot some things that insiders miss or gloss over too quickly.

The structure of the book is as follows. I discuss first the nature and the scale of the crisis in which the centre-right finds itself, and make out the general claim that the centre-right now needs a new settlement between authority and liberty, or hierarchy and individualism. I then consider four key centre-right traditions in turn and assess what each has to offer for that new settlement. They are the neo-conservative, the neo-Burkean, the political libertarian and the neo-liberal traditions. After each one, I explore a key problem that it bequeathes the next centre-right. The key problems are those of authority, nationhood and modernisation. There then follows much briefer discussion of the resources available from the North American and European centre-right traditions. I argue that the most important building block will be a new kind of deal between neo-liberalism and neo-Burkeanism. In moving from this settlement between basic political philosophies toward practical policy, I then argue that the new settlement needs to define a distinctive set of responses to risks that individuals and communities face. For it is in responding to risk that a treaty between liberty and authority has purchase and meaning for ordinary people. In particular, I argue for a more preventive stance, albeit nuanced in ways that the neo-liberal and neo-Burkean traditions require. I conclude by stating the scale of the challenge that the centre-right faces.

The current crisis of the centre-right: risks and opportunities

In May 1997, the Conservative Party suffered its biggest defeat at the polls since its defeat by Lloyd George in 1906. The immediate reasons for this were very similar to the reasons why previous Conservative governments have fallen, or indeed why governments of any party fall. Those were the problems of disloyalty; the loss of policy direction after the ejection of the pound from the EU exchange rate mechanism, which also led loss of faith in Conservatives' ability to manage the economy; loss of contact with popular feeling generally; the loss of broad appeal across class and regions, partly connected with the growing hostility of the media; weak party organisation and finances; weak public relations service; loss of support in business and in other opinion forming networks and areas of national life such as the arts and the voluntary sector; ageing membership; and the declining appeal of deference,[3] the widespread perception of sleaze and corruption, the credibility of the Labour opposition and the widespread feeling that it was time for a change.[4] But even if these problems are successfully tackled, the centre-right will not be returned to power on a credible and robust programme. The things to be done to avoid losing elections are not the same as those to be done to win them repeatedly with convincing direction for the common life of the public.

The main dimensions of the challenge for the centre-right in regaining power are well-known. The new leadership of the British Conservative party has candidly acknowledged its ageing membership, its currently limited appeal to younger people, the problems associated with its perceived arrogance, narrowly economistic goals, divisions over Britain's relationship with the continental project of European integration, and sleaze of the last Conservative government. The base in local government is still at rock bottom.

The risks presented by the agenda of New Labour are very great indeed. At a very simple level, the fact that New Labour has stolen many of the policies of the centre-right may be a threat. However, this seems to me to be the least of the problems facing the Conservative Party. There are many countries that have two leading parties in the centre ground, both with a basic orthodox macroeconomic policy, committed to sound money and tight control of public spending and to the private ownership of the broad mass of services, extraction and manufacturing and now utilities. The United States, the Republic of Ireland, New Zealand, Australia, Canada, Turkey and many other countries manage to find space for more than one party with orthodox centre-right economic policies, and there is no reason why in many parts of Britain two or three leading parties cannot compete in that arena.

Much more threatening for the centre-right in the medium term is New Labour's constitutional agenda. The Conservative and Unionist Parties will find it very hard to stomach the prospect that a Scottish Parliament and a Welsh Assembly may be unleashing the very forces for independence and separation in those nations that the party warned of during successive election campaigns. It is inconceivable that the next centre-right government in Britain will reverse whatever has become the settled position.

The very real possibility of a proportional system for general elections in the none-too-distant future raises the prospect of the pro- and anti-European wings of the Conservative party asking themselves why they remain members of the same organisation, concluding that the balance of advantage lies with schism, and then finding themselves with such a legacy of mutual loathing that they are unable to form a centre-right coalition together that could effectively govern or even attract sufficient numbers of voters that they would be given a chance to try. In such a scenario, the rise of the far right becomes frighteningly possible. Some studies of the impact of a modified alternative vote system of a kind likely to be acceptable to New Labour have projected the possibility of the Conservative Party being squeezed between a doubling of Liberal Democrat seats and an increased Labour representation. By 2001 or 2002 and, if New Labour were to win a second term, certainly by the election after that, we can expect that New Labour's share of the vote would have fallen sharply and, therefore, that they would benefit much less from such a system. But whatever the projections, the centre-right may well have to learn to operate effectively and remain united and credible within a proportional system. At a time when the Conservative Party no longer seems destined inevitably to hold a majority in England, this will be a steep cliff to climb.

There is too the possibility that by the time the party or a coalition of centre-right parties could govern in England again, the European single currency and even British membership of it will be a *fait accompli*. This is presumably most likely if the euro is a success in its early years on the continent. New Labour may do for the Conservative Party's stance on the euro what the Conservatives did for Labour on the old Clause Four, privatisation and the trades unions – make them matters on which it is futile to call for the clock to be turned back.

But there are deeper problems. For the first time since the political demise of Lloyd George, the Conservative Party no longer has a monopoly on the articulation of the interests of business. Indeed, today, the big business interest is markedly closer to New Labour, and the small manufacturing sector trading in Europe is closer to New Labour or even the Liberal Democrats. The sections of business that remain publicly and vociferously loyal to the Conservative Party tend to be smaller, in services, in the south and east, have principally domestic rather than export markets and hence are more fearful of European integration. Newer businesses, such as those operating over the Internet, often have few local or national ties and will feel little in common with a party that focuses on geographical boundaries. The latent business support is much greater, but is very hard to mobilise at a time when big businesses and the small businesses that supply them see their interests best served by pro-European economic policies that the Conservative Party today either remains hostile toward, or feels unable to express or to put forward with any conviction.

But the problem of the loss of centre-right monopoly representation is not only in respect of business interests. Mr Blair speaks of the family and local geographical community with some conviction, even if his party varies in its commitment to these things. The centre-left now has stronger roots in the arts and in networks of voluntary action than at any previous time in its history, and the centre-right must win back support in these areas as well as in business.

I shall argue that the roots of the problem for British conservatism in securing a return to power are deeper still, and that they cannot be addressed by the low politics of a better political communication, wider recruitment, more adroit élite political manoeuvre or adjustment of policy. They run much closer to the core of what conservatism, as a collection of political traditions and as a political culture, has been. While the bedrock of conservatism remains the abiding commitments of social order, private property, both authority *and* liberty, individualism *and* community, and modernisation *and* continuity, the question that I want to raise is whether conservatism, as a distinct form of the centre-right sensibility and a set of political ideas, can again make settlements between them in a way that can achieve the kind of hegemony that gave the governance of Britain to the Conservative Party for so much of the twentieth century.

Some have argued that conservatism's inheritance and traditions offer nothing to the next centre-right.[5] I do not go so far. However, it is necessary, in order to show how a revival of the centre-right might be possible, to explore and describe the conditions necessary to enable the centre-right to stage its renaissance and, at the same time, to explore the implications for the kind of centre-right that might emerge if those conditions do not come about. Conservatism, in the strict sense, may prove to be a liability, but the abiding sensibilities and impulses of centre-right will in that case be articulated in other and perhaps new ways.

But before making out this argument, it is necessary to answer those who argue that conservatism does best when it eschews intellectual debate about ideology and grand theory and focuses on statecraft, or the low politics of securing power in order to pursue the high politics of diplomacy and the interests of the social groups that conservatism naturally appeals to.[6]

There are fundamental problems with the recommendation that the centre-right should focus on 'practical politics not theory, sensibility not policy, statecraft not ideology'. Firstly, as a strategy for opposition, it is inherently of limited value, because the scope for true statecraft and political manoeuvring that is open to an opposition party is reduced to its ability to control local governments, appointed boards and other alternative sources of power in the society. However, recent Conservative governments have reduced the power of many of these institutions and, in any case, the hold over them that the Conservative party currently possesses is tenuous, albeit probably now past its nadir. Secondly, this strategy already assumes a certain kind of ideology about what conservatism stands for and where its appeal will be based. The assumption is that conservatism continues to speak with the authentic voice of certain strata of English and perhaps eventually again Scots and Welsh society, and that those strata are interested fundamentally in the efficacy of the state apparatus under the control of their natural party. But this is almost certainly no longer the case. The appeal of conservatism to business interests, to the middle class or to the aspiring working class is no more 'natural' than was socialism in its day to the public sector professionals or the skilled manual working class. Nor is it the case that the efficacy of the sovereign state has any natural appeal. Indeed, today, the appeal of these things is waning in many quarters and will not easily be restored. Thirdly and most fundamentally, the recommendation fails to recognise just where the crisis of the centre-right has arisen.

Political culture and settlements

The view of the crisis for the centre-right that I want to present is rooted in an understanding of the dynamics of political culture in societies like ours. Political culture matters enormously. For the governments that achieve lasting transformations – those of, for example, Lloyd George, Attlee, Thatcher and perhaps Blair – engage deliberately in a politics of seeking to influence the rate and the direction of change in the cultures of the public. The ambitions, not only of these leaders, but of the political projects in which they were or are engaged, have been to effect change within the weft of British society, and not merely in its current policy directions or in leading organisations.

One commonplace understanding of the change in our political culture is the idea that we have moved in recent years 'beyond left and right'. At least in the simple sense that communism and fascism have collapsed and now attract old tiny numbers of adherents in any western democracy, and to the extent that the centre-left at least in Britain has moved sharply away from the social democratic settlement to adopt many of the centre-ground positions in economic policy that once it disdained, there is some truth in this. But in many ways this is old news. It was in the second half of the 1970s that James Callaghan told the Labour Party that the opportunity for Keynesian reflation led by public expenditure in a single small European country was no longer available, and despite the siren calls in the late 1970s from some on the hard right for a genuinely authoritarian solution to the strikes, near hyperinflation, and out-of-control public spending of those years, the mainstream of the right kept firmly to the democratic path.

Moreover, the right in Britain has never been a single cultural bias or tradition, but rather a series of not always easy alliances between at least four principal traditions, which cannot themselves be ranked sensibly from soft to hard right. Political culture has, then, never been sensibly understood on a single scale. On the other hand, it does not follow that we should imagine that we can abandon all scales, or that the current triumph of the centre-left wearing some of the clothes of the centre-right means that there is no longer any space for any of the centre-right traditions. It simply means that those centre-right traditions will have to reinvent themselves, yet again.

My basic thesis is that in order to be viable – that is, not to risk extremism of the right or left or violent disruptions – societies must manage change by making constantly shifting settlements between a relatively small number of basic impulses or biases of political culture, which need to be held in a balance that becomes neither a rigid equilibrium nor a dangerous domination of one bias over all the others. A settlement is made in the first place between interest groups, factions or even between parties. But settlements that are successful permeate the wide society, and come to articulate treaties or reconciliations between values and cultures. These need not be logically consistent and will not be indefinitely durable, but they are the basis of all political projects.

Two of these fundamental impulses are those of authority and liberty, or hierarchy and individualism.[7] No society is viable that allows one of these cultural impulses to atrophy and wither. The appalling destructiveness and utter failure of the Soviet experiment provides powerful and rebarbative evidence of what befalls a society that attempts to extirpate the individualist impulse, while the well-known and tragic case of the Ik of east central Africa, documented in Colin Turnbull's famous book,[8] shows what becomes of a society that wholly abandons itself to the crude power relations of domination and fatalism, where at once individual initiative, community solidarity and the authority of law have collapsed. Where hierarchy attempts to dominate over individual aspiration and communal feeling, as Tito's Yugoslavia did, viability cannot be expected. By contrast, the success of the British state since 1660 has been the extraordinary, indeed at times uncanny, intuitive ability of its various élites, sub-élites and popular movements to find ways to shift that balance without resorting to violent insurrection or counter-insurrection – although there have been very close shaves in the 1820s and 1830s, and perhaps again in the late 1970s.

While all settlements between authority and liberty break down sooner or later, they can be relatively durable. It is this now well-documented anthropological fact about political culture that helps to explain how in democratic societies, centre-right parties have held power and secured appeal and legitimacy for so much of the twentieth century, contrary to the expectations of both radicals and old Whigs of the nineteenth century. Alliances between either of these impulses and others are, by contrast, more fragile. For the egalitarian culture waxes and wanes in sharp cycles of mobilisation and utopian effort followed by exhaustion, disappointment and schism, and fatalist cultures are poor partners with which to build political coalitions that can inspire a broad range of sensibilities.

This thesis surely holds the key to the reconstruction of the centre-right. For as we consider the conservatism of Peel, we see a treaty between the hierarchical landed interest and the individualist commercial interest. It came apart, after a generation, upon the rock of the repeal of the Corn Laws, in which the principles of economic liberty and traditional social order clashed. The rebuilding of conservatism under Disraeli is associated not only with a dynamic between 'two nations' and 'one nation', and with the acceptance of the challenge to create a future for conservatism on a wider franchise, but upon a new treaty between individualist Manchester liberalism and a sense of authority built around nationhood, monarchy and parliamentary sovereignty for which an appeal had to be created. After the debacle of 1906, conservatism flirted briefly with a hierarchical, imperial preference-based protectionism allied with some more communitarian and collective currents to which Joseph Chamberlain appealed, before returning in the 1920 to a new treaty between free trade and the strong autonomous state based on making monetary policy into an element of hierarchical high politics under the gold standard. Following the Second World War, MacMillan with his 'Middle Way' briefly attempted to span individualism in economics, a traditional conservative concern for strong central state authority and even an egalitarian commitment to the welfare state as inherited from the

Labour administration of the 1940s. Heath's attempt at Selsdon to refocus on the power diagonal between market individualism and state authority collapsed under pressure.

What was distinctive about the settlement of the Thatcher years between liberty and authority was the peculiar clarity with which the authority of the autonomous central national state was stressed, while giving greater emphasis to the individualist impulse of economic liberty than had been seen since the war. Thatcherism was not, contrary to popular punditry, pure neo-liberalism. For neo-liberalism is a deeply internationalising creed about economic freedom with genuinely globalising consequences for economic and political life, in which individual freedom to truck and barter is writ large. At the heart of Mrs Thatcher's vision stood a conception of the British nation, whether under arms in the Falklands conflict or against the European integrationist ambitions of continental social and Christian democrats. That vision of British – rather than English – national life was certainly one that sought the radical transformation of the institutions of the nation, but in no sense was it wholly comfortable with the growing interdependence of Britain that its own market opening policies – such as the single European market – brought about. Only while liberalising means served the end of the authority and the autonomy of the central British state that expressed its conception of the nation, was the Thatcherite settlement viable. The alliance between neo-liberal economics and centralising national politics with a managerial centrist style of public management was not sustainable. But it is important to explain exactly how and why that settlement unravelled.

What has come adrift in the Thatcherite settlement is not, surely, anything very much at the individualist pole of the axis. Indeed, even the centre-left in almost every western country has moved dramatically to accept the case for freer markets, entrepreneurship and greater individual responsibility for risk. The institutions for encouraging this individualism – in the forms of the World Trade Organisation, international best practice in competition policy, bankruptcy and property rights law, and the growing role of the International Standards Organisation in promoting open standards in commerce – are more secure than ever before.

Rather, the Thatcherite settlement came apart at the pole of the axis which expresses authority. Its traditional conservative ship of the strong central national state foundered between the rocks of resurgent Scottish and, to a lesser degree, Welsh nationalism and, more disastrously, on the European rocks where the contradictions between the individualist impulse to open up the single market quickly took it into the reinvigorated project for European supra-national authority, which threatened the Thatcherite commitment to the autonomy of the nation state as the central source of authority.

But a viable political culture needs to imagine two kinds of authority. State authority operates at the macro-social level, and a political project with the ambitions of conservatism has always recognised the importance of a micro-social conception of authority. Here, the Thatcherite settlement stressed the role of the family. But the rising participation of women in the labour force created major problems for this model of micro-authority, between individualists who welcomed the new and more flexible labour force and hierarchists who saw this as threatening the viability of the family, the quality of parenting and the commitment of parents to home building.

The challenge for the centre-right is to imagine and create a new settlement between these conflicting impulses of liberty and authority that can be viable in a world greatly changed from the one inherited by the conservatives who last faced this task in the late 1970s and early 1980s. In particular, the centre-right must re-imagine both micro-social and macro-social authority for the modern world. The question is whether a viable new centre-right conception of authority for the twenty-first century will have any of the distinctive characteristics of conservatism. To explore how this might be done, I turn from this general account to more specific considerations of the resources available to the centre-right from the conservative traditions for a new conception of the nature of authority.

The resources available

The conservative traditions are various. Moving within the orbit of the conservative sensibility has been an extraordinary array of ideas about authority ranging from the most outright libertarianism to the most extreme authoritarianism. Between the ideas of the Libertarian Alliance at one extreme and the authoritarianism associated with the writings of Professor Maurice Cowling of Peterhouse[9] and the early work of Roger Scruton at the other,[10] lie the more mainstream traditions.

It is worth distinguishing between two major and two minor currents and an external point of reference to which many of the traditions have looked from time to time. The two major currents may be called British neo-conservatism of the Thatcher-Major era, and a neo-Burkean strain. Neo-conservatism has been committed to securing the autonomy of the central national state from dependence upon local and supra-national bodies, and upon wider society. While its commitment to liberty and private property are undoubted, neo-conservatism's conception of the authority necessary to sustain these things has been resolutely focused upon the sovereignty of the national state. Indeed, in this tradition, the free market required the strong state, not merely because only a powerful state could push through privatisation, but because, on this view, nationalised industries had ensnared central government in industrial life in ways that could only weaken it. The smaller state was welcomed by neo-conservatives, not only for its own sake, but precisely because smaller would be stronger.[11]

The neo-Burkean current runs through some but not all of the work of the philosopher, the late Michael Oakeshott,[12] some of the writings of David Willetts on civic conservatism,[13] and the recent anti-Thatcherite tracts from Ferdinand Mount[14] and Simon Jenkins.[15] The neo-Burkean and Oakeshottian currents, along with genuinely neo-conservative ideas, have been most consistently represented and developed in the pages of the Salisbury Review and the writings of its editor, Roger Scruton.[16]

Two minor currents may also be distinguished. There is the long-standing current of libertarianism that entered conservatism slowly from the 1950s onward, in which issues of political freedom are paramount. Also, there has been a more economic outlook upon liberty that stresses economic openness and integration while being willing to accept the politically integrative consequences for pooling sovereignty: it is this which is most accurately described as 'neo-liberalism'.

Many on the left and liberal communitarians, such as the formerly conservative political philosopher John Gray, write as though this neo-liberalism was the central current within the conservative coalition of the 1980s and early 1990s.[17] In fact, the mainstream neo-conservatism of the Thatcher era was a more complex and more politically hierarchical strain, in which the autonomy of the central state from both local and supra-national sources of authority was paramount. In fact, although neo-liberal and libertarian strains have moved within the conservative sphere of gravity, if they were ever to become dominant over the neo-conservative commitment to the strong and autonomous central state or the particularist and micro-social emphasis of the neo-Burkean strain, then the result would not be conservatism in any proper sense of the word, but would a more distinctively liberal current of centre-right thought.

The external point of reference is the very different neo-conservative thought that arose in the USA in the same period, for which the leading writers are perhaps Irving Kristol,[18] the middle period Norman Podhoretz, the middle period Nathan Glazer, Jeane Kirkpatrick and Michael Novak, as well as some strands of the more complex thought of Daniel Bell[19] and Peter Berger. The journals, *Commentary* and *Encounter* provided a crucial outlet for the ideas of this current. Not consistently mined by any British tradition, this current nevertheless provided inspiration for many politicians and thinkers in several of the British conservative traditions.[20]

Figure 1. The main intellectual traditions within anglophone conservatism and their understanding of authority

Dimension of authority	UK Neo-conservatism 1975–97	Neo-Burkeanism	Political libertarianism	Internationalising neo-liberalism	US neo-conservatism 1968–95
Site of macro-social authority	Authority of autonomous central 'national' (British) state – autonomous both from other groups in society and from other national states. Sharp distinction between public sector as shpere of authority, private sector as governed	Authority of private semi-voluntary institutions sustained by norms, tradition, deference, consent, custom, common law, evolution of institutions with incremental and messy institutional creativity. No sharp distinction between public sector as authority and private sector as governed	The individual – the same as the site of liberty and the site of micro-social authority	International law of property rights underpinned by national law but buttressed ultimately by business consent	Authority of multiple tiers of local, regional, state, provincial and federal state
Core state stance toward other states, superior and inferior state structures	Machiavellian state-actor realism, statecraft, national interest and state interest identical	Negotiated partnership, concert of powers, short term core state self-interest constrained by enlightened long term self-interest	Minimal, constitutionally constrained	Cooperation, openness, intermingling, interdependence, economic integration leading politically towards shared sovereignty	Externally, Machiavellian state-actor realism, statecraft, but internally within federal republic, more negotiated partnership, concert of powers
Economic authority	Monetary policy of the autonomous national state, central control of fiscal policy: monetary and sometimes fiscal policy becomes high politics	Network of overlapping authoritative economic institutions and self-regulatory practices	Voluntarily entered agreements between individuals and firms	International property rights law	Judicially buttressed constitutional framework for private property rights
Ethics of the use of authority	Secrecy, dispatch, centralisation of statecraft necessary for efficient foreign, diplomatic, military and monetary policy	Openness can be graduated within the overlapping network of authority-sharing and authority-diffusing institutions	Transparency, minimalism	Transparency, except during trade negotiations and while adjudications are being prepared	Secrecy, dispatch and centralisation necessary only in foreign and military matters; economic policy is low politics, except in emergency, and can be quite open
Constraints upon sovereignty of principal site(s) of macro-social authority	Sovereignty of combined legislature-executive	No separation of powers, but informal separation of authorities each with functional monopoly over sphere of experience	Extreme attenuated constitutional *garantisme*	Formal pooling of sovereignty in international trade law and international definitions of property rights: radical	Constitutional *garantisme* and limited government through separation of powers

	Individual, hierarchy within firm, family	Social institution, family, voluntary association	Individual	Firm, individual consumer	Family
Site of micro-social authority	Individual, hierarchy within firm, family	Social institution, family, voluntary association	Individual	Firm, individual consumer (abridgement of autonomous national state action)	Family
Moral accountability to authority	Moral accountability principally to the autonomous central state legislature-executive	Moral accountability of all diverse institutions to one another to sustain moral life and civility	Moral accountability to other individuals, and to voluntarily entered agreements, subject to constitutional restrictions on collective action and constitutionally protected personal liberty and property rights law	Moral accountability to network of others, and to variety of overlapping institutions managing economic deregulation	Moral accountability principally of governors to constitutional order to set moral example and inculcate morality among citizens
Nature of state	State as enterprise association, with particular policy goals	State as civil association maintaining procedural rules, leaving substantive goals to particular institutions and enterprise associations	State as civil association	The inverse of mercantilism; pooling, integrating, but concerned primarily with economic goals, therefore enterprise association	Constitutional order as civil association: many tiers of statehood as enterprise associations
Legitimation appeal	Economic liberty, wealth creation, aspiration to upward economic mobility	Social cohesion and constrained political liberty within relatively fixed institutional setting of civil practices	Personal economic and lifestyle liberty	Economic liberty, wealth maximisation, prosperity	Social cohesion under authority and civil duty, economic liberty
Moral goals for citizens	General, largely negative or procedural moral goals for citizens	Community, cohesion, civility	Negative only	General, largely negative or procedural	Specific, positive substantive moral goals for citizens
Tolerance of moral diversity	Extensive under law, but limited by need to defend autonomous central state, core goals of economic liberty and wealth creation	Moderately extensive but limited by the general rules of the civil association and the rights and duties of moral subcultures as enterprise associations	Most extensive, limited only by the principle of protecting maximal possible liberty for each from the nosy preferences of others	Extensive, limited by the need to protect property rights and economic liberty from interest groups using political liberty for rent-seeking regulation or large scale public expenditure on transfers	Limited

Of course, no single politician or even political writer or thinker falls neatly for the whole of their work into just one of these traditions. Practical politicians understand very well the importance of building coalitions between currents of thought, and that excessive intellectual consistency in political ideas simply narrows the base of appeal, while serious thinkers of any subtlety appreciate the call of several contrasting impulses and sensibilities that must somehow be reconciled. Each tradition, moreover, offers some balance, however lop-sided, between its conceptions of liberty and authority.

Figure 1 (on pages 26 and 27) summarises my understanding of what each of these traditions has to say about the nature of authority.

Obviously, there have been of course, other external reference points. One, albeit briefly and in a very particularly British neo-conservative interpretation, was the 1950s German social market theory of Ludwig Erhard.[21] More rarely, German Christian Democracy served as reference point, with its commitment to subsidiarity, federalism, European integration and a foreign policy based upon détente and the concert of powers rather than the ruthless realism of autonomous nation states. However, even among the pro-European strains of British conservatism, this was probably a very minor current. In general, British pro-Europeans such as Sir Leon Brittan and Lord Cockfield have tended – whether rightly or misguidedly is still being debated – to welcome European integration in the hope that it would reinforce an internationalising neo-liberalism rather than a Christian Democratic enclave. As with libertarianism and internationalising neo-liberalism, if a Christian Democratic strain became dominant, the result would no longer be conservatism (at least, in the British sense), for the social Catholic interest in corporatist forms of organisation, the rejection of any special status in the hierarchy of authority for the national state and the insistence on subsidiarity in the structure of governance are quite foreign to English neo-conservatism[22] – although perhaps they have resonances with some Scots conservative traditions.

What, then, can these various traditions offer the centre-right today in the effort to imagine a new conception of authority that will be both relevant to the twenty-first century and acceptable to the cohorts for whom the last conservative settlement on authority seems to hold a declining appeal?

The neo-conservative inheritance

I have argued that the main neo-conservative current's stress on the autonomous central British state and the family based on full-time parenting has already failed to offer the kind of conception of authority on which the centre-right can rebuild a coalition that will return it to power with the consent of many younger cohorts.

The key point here is that during the Thatcher years, there emerged a very particular settlement between the impulses to liberty and authority. Between the goal of wealth and prosperity with its associated neo-liberal commitment to economic liberty and the goal of the autonomy and power of the central state, there emerged a fragile treaty in which each could be seen as the means of achieving the other. In order to secure economic liberty, a strong core central state was needed to face down the trades unions and the entrenched commitment of the bureaucracy and segments of the population to regulation and state ownership. Conversely, the agenda of economic liberty required the divestment of the burdens of nationalised industry, while deregulation of capital and flows would free the state to pursue high politics. The appeal of monetarism to neo-conservatives was not purely or even principally economic, although it certainly appeared in the late 1970s to have the makings of a powerful tool with which to combat inflation, albeit at the price of very high unemployment. Rather, its real appeal was political. The making of austere monetary policy itself into high politics – both above the hurly-burly of interest group and domestic factional politics, and central to the conduct of independent foreign policy through interest rate policy – enabled the reassertion of both the authority of the national state and the liberty of entrepreneur to co-exist in the bracing climate of monetary discipline.[23]

Many on the centre-right want to believe that this relationship between authority and liberty can be re-created. My argument is that it cannot. 'Thatcherism in one country' was as absurd and self-contradictory an ambition as any found in the capitalist world. It was sustainable for its moment precisely because the economic and political world of the British isles the 1980s was much less integrated and interdependent with the rest of the world and especially with Europe than today.

The analogy was often drawn by those who imagined that Thatcherism in one country could be made viable that Britain could be to Europe what Hong Kong has been for eastern Asia. But the argument behind the analogy cannot be sustained. A maritime city state can indeed, at least for a while, be an entrepôt within a climate of economic growth and widespread protectionism in the surrounding region. The British Isles, however, have a much larger population, are now surrounded by much more open markets and must earn their livings in a more diverse range of ways than a maritime city state needs to. Moreover, the nature of the region with which the British Isles are involved has been very different, politically and economically, from eastern Asia. The European project, of which Britain is now irreversibly a part, has no east Asian analogue. The same detached role is simply not available. Detachment from the European project would not occur – assuming that British business and the international money, gilts and stocks markets would tolerate such a policy at all – without loss of market access. Moreover, as successive US ambassadors to Britain have made clear, Britain's influence in Washington, such as it is, depends almost entirely on its continued role within the European Union. The World Trade Organisation would not be able to enforce British access to European markets after Britain had departed the Union, even if should want to enter the European Economic Area along with Norway and Switzerland. The flight of capital and skilled labour, and the loss of influence in the United States and on the UN Security Council that are involved in the 'Hong Kong of Europe' strategy would be too great for any future centre-right government to contemplate, even if it nostalgically considered the option ideally desirable.

Moreover, it was the neo-liberal strain within the Thatcherite settlement – resulting in the removal of exchange controls, the creation of the single market by 1992 following the Single European Act of 1986 and a host of other deregulatory policy initiatives – that helped to bring about that integration and interdependence. The autonomy of the central state is worth something when autonomy has a jurisdiction over which its policy instruments can be effective. That clear economic jurisdiction has been blurring and dissolving steadily since 1979. With it, the nature of effective authority has shifted.

The nineteenth century origins of the neo-conservative conception of the nation state as the source of authority place a Palmerstonian emphasis upon the central state's right of unilateral action in foreign policy, while the late Victorian constitutional thought from Dicey onward began to stress, in the vocabulary of parliamentary sovereignty, that same autonomy in domestic affairs.[24] In the conditions of the post-war world, this tradition has become something of a liability. Unilateral action in foreign policy can provoke as much distrust as awe, as the United States has persistently found. Moreover, in much of the developed world, it is precisely through the pooling of powers to act in concert through international law, the United Nations and other bodies, and by way of treaties permitting mutual surveillance, that trust and peace are maintained. Where secrecy, despatch and independence are the principal, rather than the subordinate, armamentarium of states today, we usually observe uncivil societies.[25] For a country firmly committed within NATO, the EU and the WTO to imagine that autonomy in foreign policy is still a principal virtue is not merely to send inaccurate signals but to court isolation and even retaliation, as both Greece and France have found to their cost. Similarly, for a central state to imagine that it can act independently of local and domestic interests and plural sources of authority over long periods of time is to run acute risks of depriving itself of vital intelligence and capacity, and, more importantly, to take grave risks with its own legitimacy. The age of interdependence in governance is one in which the autonomous central state is of declining usefulness.

Turning to the micro-social level of authority, the even more intransigent 'family values' authoritarianism of the US neo-conservative tradition, rooted, as it typically is, in the authority of revealed religion, seems even less likely to be a successful transplant than is a revived assertion of Thatcherite 'Victorian values' or Majorite 'back to basics'. To be sure, most children are indeed still brought up in two parent households, and as people live longer, those marriages that survive the first ten years (when most divorces occur) are themselves more long lived than ever. The 'traditional' family – though the centre-right ought to be careful to acknowledge that the tradition, like many, is relatively recent one and is therefore the more mutable – is not dead, nor necessarily dying.

But it is certainly changing. While many remain monogamous throughout parenthood and even throughout life, growing numbers are choosing serial monogamy. But the big driver of change is not simply permissiveness in sexual behaviour: if that were all, then it would be as readily reversible within a generation as was the Regency laxity by the mid-Victorian age.

The 'Taliban tendency'[26] in the centre-right that seeks to use the authority of the state to enforce monogamy, heterosexuality, parental authority over children and censorship of the media on the portrayal of sex, and to penalise abortion, discourage divorce, cohabitation and illegitimacy and other deviations from what it regards as the family norm, is now an electoral liability. The point is not that there are huge numbers of gay men and lesbians, or that cohabitation and divorce are now normal behaviour: they are not. Rather, the point is that among those who continue to form traditional families, socially liberal attitudes are now far more widespread than are micro-socially authoritarian ones: indeed, they are the norm.

The fundamental changes in family life are economic, and centre upon the economic activity, power and autonomy of women. All this is good news to neo-liberals concerned not only about wealth creation but about competition in labour markets, greater flexibility in working arrangements and wider bases of skills throughout the population. There are no examples in history of societies that have effectively reversed – or even consistently *aspired* to reverse – such fundamental change. The challenge for the centre-right in micro-social matters is not to bend with the wind, to accept change, to make the best of what is. Rather, it is to imagine afresh how the changing household arrangements can be part of a new settlement between liberty and authority.

For while family life is changing, authority is already being rein-vented, albeit with difficulty. New norms of integrity and duty between partners have emerged, as the sillier aspects of sexual irre-sponsibility by a marginal few twenty or 30 years ago fade from memory. The duty, for example, of fathers to support children even when the relationship between the parents had ended, is now almost universally accepted: coarse libertinism is now defended by hardly anyone. As this has become accepted, a new ethic of duty for the age of serial monogamy has begun to be developed, albeit with difficulty and conflict. More negotiated and consent-based forms of authority within the family have begun to emerge that may prove more robust than were the norms of parental *fiat* and punishment. As many young people live within the parental home much later into their twenties, new forms of inter-generational responsibility are emerging, in which duties for young people partially to support themselves and meet at least part of the costs of their keep are accepted.

Nevertheless, one key element of British neo-conservative thought about authority remains convincing and an important legacy to the next centre-right. This is the wholesale rejection of the idea of Oakeshott and many neo-Burkeans that the state can legitimate itself, even with the élites, without having specific purposes.[27] British neo-conservatism was certainly astute enough to recognise that popular consent for any centre-right project, even – and perhaps especially – among the better off, would not be forthcoming just by setting ground rules for the constitution and for the exchange of private property and then allowing people to pursue their own goals. The point is not simply that the Thatcher administrations were relentlessly committed to such middle class welfare programmes as subsidised higher education and home ownership, but the more fundamental one that people expect the state to deliver on *policies* before they will support a political project. No political project that confines itself to constitutional rule-making is credible to a people that expects government to make efforts – at the very least – to reduce crime, to create the climate for wealth creation and the creation of employment, to drive up educa-tional achievement and to improve health, and latterly to nurture prac-tical commitment to environmental quality.[28] A state that pursues these things has clear and specific purposes, but only by at least doing this can its authority hope to be secured with the public. The irony here is that while the peculiar settlement between neo-conservatism and neo-liberalism of the 1980s turned itself – and Britain – once and for all against mercantilist protectionism, it secreted within itself the ancient mercantilist conception of the developmental state that pursues first and always economic advantage and wealth.

To be sure, there are dangers here. To risk the legitimacy of a whole political project upon the success of particular economic or social policies is to endanger liberty, democracy and civility themselves, should conditions turn adverse or should errors of policy be made.[29] Yet there is no credible constitutionalist alternative that can command authority.

The challenge for authority

Like many people who are not conservatives, I long found the libertarian and neo-liberal currents within the centre-right more interesting than the authoritarian ones. Indeed, only a few Peterhouse extremists would today bear the label 'authoritarian' with pride, and then, one suspects, principally *pour épater le bourgeois*. (However, some US neo-conservatives, at least during the Cold War, went out of their way to advocate a foreign policy of support for authoritarian regimes in so many words, albeit principally as bulwarks against communism and for lack of democratic alternatives to support in that capacity, and also arguing that authoritarian regimes of the right are preferable to communist ones, when there is no other alternative.)[30] In general, the genuinely conservative current on the centre-right – as opposed to the libertarian and neo-liberal traditions – has preferred to distinguish a positive conception of authority from the totalising and oppressive character of authoritarianism. Indeed, I shall argue, the contribution that the abiding commitments of the centre-right brings to democratic culture is exactly this. Like the value of many of the promised commitments of the centre-left, the positive role of authority remains unredeemed, but the political aspiration continues.

Authority is important to conservatives for a number of reasons. Firstly, in the conservative imagination it is the manager of basic social risk.[31] By inculcating self-discipline and hence responsible balanced self-hood, community and stable reproduction of the species and the community, authority sustains the basic institutions that manage risk in any society. The images of social life in the absence of authority that occur to conservatives are ones of violence, arbitrary and random individual violations of rights and duties, the undermining of cultures of morality and duty, the corrosion of incentives to build, save, work, invest, cooperate and compete and therefore the undermining of order and prosperity.[32] The fatalistic strain in the conservative imagination takes these fears to be hardly mutable facts about human nature and the disorders that, without authority, it would be heir to. Authority is, in this conception, the giver of guarantees and basic physical protection against social violation – this was the origin of the state.[33]

Secondly, authority is one of the major vehicles of purpose in social life. Oakeshott's conception of the state solely as a purely civil association without specific positive purposes, but only negative purposes in setting procedural rules, is therefore an interloper from liberalism. For in the neo-conservative tradition, the authority of the state may not be specific and positive in the sense that the mercantilists aspired to, with the state pursuing national wealth, but it remains specific and positive in that in pursues the nurturing of social order (as opposed to either chaos or social equality), economic prosperity and property.[34]

Thirdly, authority provides the means by which individuals are socially recognised. The egalitarian impulse that seeks recognition for the lowest and poorest is one that erodes the recognition of individual difference, which authority endlessly resurrects. The means of recognition by authority are rewards and sanctions, role and ritual, acclaim and shame, and, underlying all this, classification.[35] In systems of personal authority, the leader provides the categories by which classification of merit, effort or other socially valued activity is done. In more abstract systems of the authority of 'laws not men' or 'rules not roles', institutions do the classifying, and the authority of those who steer the institutions rests on their office in the institutional structure.[36]

For these purposes, authority requires power. Neo-conservatism departs from authoritarianism in rejecting the true reactionary's claim that authority fails unless everyone in society stands in constant fear, awe and shame before authority.[37] The conservative proximity to and rapprochement with liberalism has been on the idea that legitimacy rests eventually not on mystified, ascribed grounds – such as dynastic inheritance or revealed religion – but on consent, in which those subjected to authority accept it on the basis that it delivers its valued functions but remains in some way accountable to them, even if not transparent in every regard, lest transparency undermine efficacy. Authority's face of terror– the neo-conservative affirms against the reactionary – need be turned against only the recalcitrant and wicked minority who have turned to crime.

The true authoritarian is a simplifier of power. The authoritarianism of the dictator is to imagine the counterbalancing forces, separate powers and institutional nexus of diffused interacting authority valued or even romanticised by Burkeans to be merely weeds in which the simplifying arbitrariness of the decision maker can be snared if they are not cleared away.[38]

But here emerges the instability of the neo-conservative tradition. Where the Burkean recognises the importance of the careful plurality of institutional life and the disciplining of power with powers, the neo-conservative insistence on the autonomy of the central state, and on the importance of independence from other sources of authority both within and outside the territory, runs the risk of collapsing into authoritarianism.

The challenge for the next centre-right is to begin to define a conception of authority, for which practical institutional arrangements can be found, that will be viable for the new society and economy and can both perform these social functions and be legitimate with people from cohorts much younger than today's typical Conservative Party members or activists. The neo-conservative tradition alone offers too few resources for this and therefore, we must look to the other traditions of the centre-right.

The seductions of Edmund Burke

The neo-Burkean tradition is described in Figure 1 in a peculiarly pure form. Because I have tried very deliberately to disentangle it from neo-conservatism in order to present its distinctive fundamental logic, many conservatives who like to think of themselves as Burkeans will not recognise it. Certainly, that protean and splendidly self-contradictory thinker, Burke himself, would not have recognised this reduction as anything more than a caricature of one element of the middle period of his work, after his Rockingham Whiggery had been abandoned and before his descent into blunt and crude authoritarian reaction in his last years.[39] But no matter. The point is to identify the distinctive logic of the 'little platoons' and 'mediating institutions' argument in order to specify an account of authority.

The neo-Burkean tradition has never succeeded in becoming the dominant strain of thought about authority on the centre-right, precisely because of the enduring power of the neo-conservative commitment to the strong and autonomous central state. Neo-Burkeans who have wanted to make the case for more autonomous local government, universities, schools and voluntary associations have used a variety of rhetorics with which to make their appeal to the centre-right sensibilities. A common one[40] is to appeal to a pristine and authentic ancient constitution, supposedly vandalised by the centralising instincts of a statist executive with which conservatism has compromised too much and too long. Unfortunately, the historical validity of the claim that there was a historical period when a range of institutions in England had such a high degree of autonomy from the central state is suspect. Local government has always been a creature of state, and the courts have regarded private charity as limited in scope to that which the state could administer, if the trustees defaulted.[41]

Another argument is to stress the groundedness of economic relations in social structure and culture, which can only be engendered by the continuing innovation of a variety of mediating institutions,[42] in order to secure their vitality. Fundamentally, neo-Burkean ideas represent a deeper rupture with both neo-conservative and internationalising neo-liberal sensibilities about the nature of authority than many neo-Burkeans have been willing publicly to admit.

The neo-Burkean tradition remains an available resource for the centre-right, but in order for it to be developed into a coherent account of micro-social and macro-social authority, it will have to be developed into a much more rounded account of the limits to central state autonomy and the nature of any protections from dissolution under market competition to be offered to mediating institutions, and it must acknowledge the price that will have paid for this.

More than this, the neo-Burkean commitment to the vitality of mediating institutions must be freed from the genuinely Burkean idea – which I shall call paleo-Burkean – that the really valuable mediating institutions are the ancient ones.[43] For in order to make the neo-Burkean idea appeal to the modernising cultures of younger cohorts in Britain, it must be acknowledged that the most effective, legitimate and powerfully innovative and socially appealing mediating institutions are often new or recent ones. Many longstanding British mediating institutions may lack exactly the loyalty, innovation and capacity for social renewal that neo-Burkeans claim to value. Neo-Burkeans tend to worry about the extension of the principles of market-led creative destruction to established institutions, and yet such institutions are often as dependent upon these processes for their social and cultural force as firms are.

For here is exhibited in its clearest form the contemporary problem with the Burkean imagination of authority. The paleo-Burkean conception of mediating institutions relied heavily upon deferential and subaltern forms of popular participation in mediating institutions. Churches, universities, schools, voluntary bodies and local authorities are expected, in paleo-Burkean thought, to regulate behaviour authoritatively and to command loyalty and commitment on the basis of the charisma of their antiquity and mystified efficacy. To cohorts that have experienced very high levels of mass education, that have come to expect flatter hierarchies and more consultative management practice in the work place, to aspire to more intellectually challenging forms of work and greater levels of general social mobility, and have learned more open and reasoning forms of parenting, the kinds of authority that inspire consent are those that offer some opportunity for reasoned dialogue, redress and, when all else fails, participation. The very social contract thinking between current parties that Burke sometimes derided as a travesty of the civic life has become the condition upon which little platoons attract and retain members.[44]

The most important resource bequeathed to the next-centre-right by the neo-Burkeans is the recognition, indeed the commitment, to pluralism in the imagination of authority. It is worth recalling that Burke thought of himself for much of his life as a Whig, and it is from some strains of the Whig tradition that are descended the pluralistic conception of authority expressed at Philadelphia in 1787 in the separation of powers and the interdependence of the tiers of the state and of civil society. Burke condemned the French revolution for its centralism and violence, but largely approved the American revolution for its continuity with the Whig tradition that he continued, however ambiguously, to inhabit. In this, neo-Burkean sensibilities break most critically with the neo-conservative commitment to the autonomy of the central state, and offer the next generation on the centre-right something of enormous value.

But there is a second element in the neo-Burkean inheritance that may prove a valuable resource for the next centre-right. It is almost impossible to give credence to any account of the politics of the new century in which a viable settlement between the claims of environmentalism and the interests of both business and the less economically well-off is not urgently demanded and central to politics. The centre-left's vocabularies of 'sustainable development' have hitherto not demonstrated that they can map out a viable settlement. If the centre-right is address this issue credibly, then it can at least reach for the neo-Burkean ideas of contract and duty between generations. 'Conservation' may have been a narrow and perhaps patrician conception of environmentalism. But the basic Burkean idea is sound, that we owe to future generations good stewardship of resources that our descendants are almost sure to want, whatever technologies we can imagine them developing. More important still, perhaps, is the fact that the neo-Burkean tradition may be better able than many other centre-right traditions to give grounding for the conception of risk that must underlie any credible settlement between environmental concerns and commitments to economic growth – namely, that certain risks ought to be prevented.[45] Certainly, no other centre-right tradition offers any similar recognition with which to address the environmental challenge.

The ambivalence of national sentiment

Tensions over nationhood are at the heart of both the centre-right's political and intellectual problems. This is why the issue of European integration has become so divisive.

The Eurosceptic coalition is surprisingly broad, because some people in each of the four main conservative traditions have found reasons for either permanent or temporary alliance with it. Neo-conservatives fear Europe as a threat to the autonomy of the nation state and, in particular, to that most autonomous element in the nation state, central government. Those attracted to US-style neo-conservatism tend to be opposed, not because they fear that an integrated Europe will succeed, but because they feel that it will fail. Neo-Burkeans have feared the sheer size of the Brussels machine and some have been persuaded that it represents a centralising and homogenising force, riding roughshod over the plurality of sources of authority that they cherish. Political libertarians object principally to the specific content of the economic policy that has been espoused by the Commission and indeed, the Council of Ministers, under the influence of continental social and Christian democrats. While most internationalising neo-liberals have tended to be pro-European as long as they could see in the Union an instrument for the negotiation of global free trade deals, those who saw it as committed to a neo-Gaullist 'fortress Europe' strategy, despite the best efforts of Sir Leon Brittan, have been enticed into Euro-scepticism. Of these four traditions, only the hardline British neo-conservatives need to be committed permanent Eurosceptics, whatever the European Union actually does. If the EU were ever to be serious about a 'Europe of the regions', variable geometries and the devolution of all kinds of power both to and beneath the nation state, and to building a series of *ad hoc* coalitions between many tiers of authority in the name of subsidiarity, some neo-Burkeans might be won round. Similarly, if the EU adopted wholly free trading and deregulatory economic policies, libertarians and the Eurosceptic neo-liberals would be open to persuasion.

Even with these basic positions, there might have been room for manoeuvre on strategy and tactics. In the first half of the Thatcherite period, it was just possible to adopt traditional neo-conservative tactics of statecraft, basically to obstruct from within. This was possible only as long as the market opening agenda of 1992 united both neo-liberals and the business interests they were able to articulate with those neo-conservatives who could see strategic advantage in a political role for Britain in Europe. However, faced with the integrationist statecraft of Delors and his allies and successors, and with the closing of the era when neo-liberal internationalising means could still serve the ends of the autonomous central national state, this strategy failed. Mrs Thatcher's famous Bruges speech was a recognition of this, but in the place of statecraft, neo-conservatism could only offer fundamental opposition. During the Major years, consensus could not be achieved, either on fundamental position or on strategy, with the consequence that fundamental opposition became more shrill and less efficacious, and the exercise of statecraft became less convincing in Europe as it became clear that it could not carry conviction within the Conservative Party in Britain. In opposition and faced with a Blair government that has every incentive to keep the issue of European monetary union alive for as long as possible in order to prolong the divisions on the centre-right and the possibility that the euro may be a *fait accompli* by the time New Labour loses power, statecraft is not an option and fundamental opposition is at best a stop gap. Meanwhile, few voters find anti-Europeanism to be of direct relevance and the constituency for which this is the central political issue is very small indeed.

It is high time for the centre-right to consider afresh the role that its various strands want nationhood to perform. Again, it is sensible to start by assessing the resources offered by the inherited political traditions and sensibilities.

Neo-conservative and neo-Burkean tradtions each have their own conception of why nationhood matters and, within the British Isles, just which nation matters. For the neo-conservative, nationhood is the basis of the legitimacy of the central state, and the ground of its autonomy. In that tradition, the sentiment of nationhood is not merely the rationale for central power – popular support for the Queen's head upon the coinage provides the basis for the state to exercise central control over the money supply – but the basis of obedience to authority and the organisation of interests and projects in the wider world. The neo-Burkean sees nationhood less as a relationship between citizen and centre or a duty to further the interests of the state than as the sharing in a certain kind of experience. That experience is seen as often local, particularistic and — to the paleo-Burkean — traditional, to be found through involvement in local chapters of organisations that express nationhood, in commitment to the larger national culture. The national distinctiveness and vibrant organic plurality of the national culture matters more to the neo-Burkean than does the capacity of the central state that prosecutes high politics in the name of the nation. Where the neo-conservative is instrumental about nationhood, seeing it through the lens of authority, the neo-Burkean is romantic, viewing it through the spectacles of shared life in organic institutions. It is not surprising, then, that where neo-Conservatives have been concerned with Britain and its power to 'punch above its weight', neo-Burkeans feel for England and the cultures of its countryside, towns and cities, and find there strands of common identity that rise above the fissiparous bonds of religion, ethnicity, race, local or civic pride alone. The neo-conservative view is a universal claim about the powers and authority of nation states, more akin to that of the old liberal, Woodrow Wilson, than to particularistic and confined sensibilities of neo-Burkean political practice.

I have argued already that the neo-conservative conception is of declining usefulness. Does it follow that the centre-right can therefore simply accept the neo-Burkean offer? Indeed, will the prospect, delivered by New Labour, of a Scottish parliament that may yet dissolve the Act of Union, reinvigorate English identity in ways that can revive the things for which the neo-Burkean hopes?

Not necessarily. The paleo-Burkean ideal of a national experience in which tradition, ancient institutions and ancestral loyalties dominate the sensibility of nationhood is perhaps least likely to be available. For both Britain and England have been for almost two centuries, countries in which innovation in culture, technologies, sciences, institutions and arts have been central ambitions. 'The tradition of the new' is much more deeply rooted in the British Isles than has been recognised by those who ascribe it to the shallow banalities of 1960s 'swinging London'. Modernisation, too, is a tradition, and it was as much at the heart of Victorian engineering and institutional creativity in the construction of local government, as it has been in the arts, where Rennie Mackintosh in Scotland and Moore and the St Ives group in England or Birtwhistle today have all expressed a tradition at least as British, Scottish or English as the nostalgic lyricism of Elgar, or Nicholas Maw and John Piper today. The 1990s dance scenes are as English as the nostalgias of Britpop for an reinvented 1960s are British. English and British culture both have been characterised by volatility, restlessness and impatience, and often by a irreverent satirical or self-mocking comedy that cannot appeal to the paleo-Burkean.

In addition, English and British cultures are at once mongrel and magpie. Not only in imperial times but in the post-war age of open and international culture exchange, we have been as quick to borrow and adapt as to lend, from North America, from Asia and from continental Europe. The features that no one can credibly claim for the cultures of the British Isles are those of being autochthonous or exhibiting that sterile degeneration of the virtue of integrity that comes from mining only one's own roots.[46]

A key question is what relationship such a project would have with a new conception of micro-social and macro-social authority. For one who identifies herself or himself with the modern and mutually conflicting cultures of their mongrel and magpie nation will not today typically adopt that stance toward national authority which says 'my nation-state, right or wrong', but may on occasion feel the patriotism of dissent. Still less will such a modern involvement with the cultures of these islands, recognising their necessary openness to cultural trade and rapid cultural change, naturally lead to any aspiration for cultural autonomy and national borders or sovereignty over the experience of national cultural life. The paleo-Burkean and the neo-conservative could once settle upon a politics in which national life should be expressed in a bond of obedience to the authority and autonomy of the nation state. No longer.

The neo-Burkean understanding of the plurality of authority is now most effectively matched with the neo-liberal recognition that while states are inter-dependent, managing that inter-dependence crucially depends upon the building of plural but mutually consistent sources of international legal authority for business and social lives for many more people that are ever less bounded by frontiers. To the extent that the European Union can be used as a resource from which to build outwards, it should be the goal of the next centre-right to use it for that purpose, and to marginalise the European protectionist agenda that still lurks in many corners of Brussels politics.

European monetary union may or may not be a success by 2005. If it is a failure, it is probable that there will be no attempt to resurrect it for a generation – just as it took 25 years from the collapse of the attempt to create a single currency following the Werner report of 1970 to make the present effort. If it is a success and if Britain were to enter early with business and popular support, then the centre-right would have to come to terms with the fact. What is really at issue here is the neo-conservative commitment to the pound as symbol of central state autonomy to devalue if necessary, and to pursue monetary politics as statecaft and high politics wherever useful.

However, it would be quite wrong to imagine that the euro will in practice be the sole currency in Europe, or even in Britain if the British state takes its own currency into it. In practice, there are – unleashed by the neo-liberal agenda – for the first time now many powerful private currencies that could grow to account for very significant proportions of transactions in the British isles over the next few years. These include air miles, the loyalty points schemes of many retail consortia, new Internet-based currencies and many more.[47] If in ten years time, say, ten per cent of transactions are denominated in private currencies, and many business-to-business transactions are denominated in euros, it is quite possible that there will grow up in Britain a much more instrumental attitude to currency. In that situation, it would quite possible for the centre-right not merely to find a way to accept the existence of the euro, if it had proven a success, or even to accept British membership, but positively to develop the neo-liberal agenda for the growth of private commercial currencies as a distinctive policy stance. In this way, a neo-Burkean commitment to plural sources of authority can be allied with a neo-liberal agenda for markets in money.

The issue of nationhood has been central not merely *vis-à-vis* Europe but in the ambitions of conservative unionism for the relationship between the countries within the British Isles. A central question about the cultural foundations of a revived neo-Burkean project is whether it can embrace and articulate for a centre-right political sensibility the very aspects of English, Scots and perhaps still of British culture that have appealed least to the conservative cultural disposition. It seems to me that there are good reasons for optimism here. The centre-right has at various times, and most especially in the second half of the nineteenth century, been able to articulate an outward-looking, questioning and modernising sensibility of how the national culture might grow, borrow and become.

By the time the centre-right regains power, New Labour's devolution and proportional representation plans as well as other sources of changes in political culture will have brought about profound changes in these relationships. Unionism has a declining appeal in Scotland, and in England many people who might consider voting Conservative are now relaxed even about Scottish independence. Unfortunately, the decline in membership and 1997 defeat have left the Conservative Party with both a rump membership and a parliamentary representation that is quite disproportionately disposed to unionism and, when at bay, perhaps even English nationalism. But a strategy of wrapping the centre-right in the flag of St. George will alienate many more than it will attract.

If some federal solution begins to emerge within Britain, the centre-right will need to accept it and work with it if only for the simple reason of recognising political reality.[48] It is quite possible both to do this and to make the case for reducing the costs of expensive and excessive governance. The challenge is to demonstrate how a lean and efficient federal system could be made to work. But even if, at some stage, there were to be a separate English parliament, there will both real dangers and few opportunities for the centre-right to flirt with English nationalism. Firstly, this will have no appeal to business constituencies that will need to operate increasingly across frontiers. Secondly, as many more people have families and networks of friends and acquaintances that cross boundaries not only within the British Isles but beyond, a 'little England' agenda has no purchase on their experience or their aspirations. Whatever the constitutional relationship between England and Scotland or Wales, the word 'independence' will never capture the real degree of social, economic, cultural and political involvement that in practice the countries of these islands will have with each other. English nationalism will seem merely imperialistic and offensive at a time when more constructive politics will be needed, and when some of the centre-right's capacities for institutional creativity will be most needed. For the centre-right to pay most attention to its current English nationalist and die-in-a-ditch unionist rump of members and politicians who are wholly unrepresentative of its potential electoral support will not merely be a tactical and electoral mistake, but a profound miscalculation of the viable directions available for its future. If the federal option were to fail, and if Scottish elections or any future referendum clearly indicate that some threshold has been crossed, the centre-right should enable a 'velvet divorce' to be as amicable, constructive and sensibly conducted as possible. Thereafter, the task of rebuilding the centre-right within Scotland on its native, liberal Scottish Enlightenment roots will be a great deal easier.

The Cheshire Cat of libertarianism

Political libertarianism has been, I argue, the smile of the conservative Cheshire Cat. Its rhetoric has been invaluable, not only because it balances the classical conservative commitment to the autonomous central state but because it articulates politically the cultural appeal of that economic neo-liberalism with which neo-conservatism has allied itself since the 1970s. I do not mean to suggest that libertarianism was or is a mere figleaf over a basic authoritarian project. While neo-Burkeans complain of authoritarianism in the 1980s,[49] the degree of authoritarianism represented by the breaking of the miner's strike, the abolition of the Greater London Council and the erosion of the powers of the rest of local government is of a rather different order from that of regimes in Latin America or the Middle East conventionally regarded as authoritarian.

Nevertheless, the ambitions of libertarianism for the radical individualisation of responsibility for risk were not and could not be realised in a neo-conservative project which depended on the socialisation of those costs that the middle classes remained committed to – much of medicine, a large slice of education, a continuing safety net of income maintenance and even a portion, albeit declining, of the costs of home ownership (as Prime Minister, Mrs Thatcher took the view that mortgage income tax relief, albeit a cost to the exchequer, was a politically vital benefit). Political libertarians within the centre-right coalition also felt ambivalent about much of the law and order agenda – reassured by the tough protection of property rights, alarmed by some of the changes in police powers and procedures.

It is far from my purpose to defend libertarianism. Like many people (on both right and left), I feel its visceral attraction but find its assumptions about a viable society incredible and fear some of its risks. Political libertarianism is a creature of romantic politics and, in that sense, always a strange interloper in the dry-eyed and ruthless world of high politics which is the neo-conservative ambition. Even its relations with the humdrum and unromantic materialism of economic neo-liberalism are not wholly cordial: the civic well-springs of political liberty are not the same as the prosperity-hungry and entrepreneurial ones of economic liberty. The ideal that the site and source of liberty and of micro-social authority should be one and the same is, while beautiful and appealing, simply incredible. Individuality and individualism are social practices only possible in a society of organisations, in a certain complex and common culture, in certain kinds of social network configurations and in a certain institutional context of authority. The renewal of that organisational, cultural and institutional setting requires forces that libertarianism cannot assemble. Moreover, the means by which the libertarian goal of a society of self-reliance and individual responsibility for risk could be achieved would involve a hugely strong state. For this could be initiated and sustained only if the state were strong enough at once to disengage with popular aspirations for protection, and capable of persuading a sceptical citizenry that they ought to wish to shoulder these hitherto socialised burdens. Moroever, such a state would have to be capable of assaulting all the institutions (often ones beloved of neo-Burkeans) that not only sustain the pooling of risk, but may also make possible a confident and grounded individualism. For, in some measure, the education systems and the teaching and research professions, much of the world of modern charity, the medical profession and even some parts of the benefit system support modern individuality. Faced with the determination of neo-conservatives and neo-Burkeans to contain it, what can libertarianism offer the next centre-right?

Certainly, the articulation – if not in the libertarian form – of the abiding impulse to political liberty will have, in my view, to become more central to the next right than it was to the last. Political liberty has many expressions, and it will serve the centre-right ill to imagine that they have already been fulfilled in the British Isles in as many ways as are desirable.

One dimension is that of political participation. The Blairite centre-left has for the moment made much of the running here, with its experiments in referenda on constitutional change and some marginal use of citizens' juries and even deliberative polls. But in other parts of the world, the extension of political participation is part of a centre-right agenda: there are few louder supporters of wider political participation in the USA than Speaker of the House of Representatives Newt Gingrich and right-wing talk radio host Rush Limbaugh. Indeed, within the narrow confines of the encouragement of balloting in trades unions over strikes, more popular participation was part of the agenda of the Thatcher governments. The neo-conservative nostrum that participation should be encouraged only when the fickle vicissitudes of public opinion currently favour its own positions is a dangerous one today. For since the 1960s and 1970s, three fundamental facts have changed about the distribution of political power and knowledge that leave this Machiavellianism of high politics exposed. The first is rising educational achievement – to which the expansion of higher education since the late 1980s is making an enormous contribution. The second is the rise in the power, range, scrutiny and intrusiveness of the media, while the third is the growth in interactive media from the simple phone-in to the Internet and new techniques of deliberative polling. However, the challenge for any viable agenda for managing the expansion of public participation in political decision making is to prevent the capture of participation opportunities by vested interests by the fashionable or influential pressure groups of the day, or indeed by organisations that are in fact dominated by party patronage.

The philosophical commitment of libertarianism to political participation is, of course, constrained. Its support for the expression of opinion and the right to participate is clear, but the libertarian seeks constitutional guarantees that would prevent collective decision making on the back of such participation that would lead to socialising risk or property beyond that which is necessary for the minimal state.[50] The evident cultural unviability of such a position means that other traditions within the centre-right will have to shoulder the responsibility of articulating a new populist radicalism about political participation, if its attractions are to be seized from the centre-left.

A second strand of political liberty is concerned with civil liberties with regard to the judicial role of the state. The neo-conservative tradition tends to see any extension of the claims of civil liberties as undermining the authority necessary for the detection and punishment of crime, and points to the rising popular support for tough action on criminals and the rising numbers reporting themselves in surveys as willing to see the ending of rights to silence and even of the traditional commitment that it is better that a guilty person go free than that an innocent person be unjustly punished.[51] Nevertheless, there are real dangers for the centre-right here. Linear extrapolations of trends are always dangerous, especially with regard to trends in public opinion. Moreover, the social composition of those whose conception of authority suggests to them that civil liberties represent a threat to order is ageing and highly skewed both geographically and in terms of the larger potential centre-right electorate. Moreover, even within public opinion on law and order, there are more complex currents, including a rising interest in forms of diversion, prevention and even rehabilitation (that last was once, it should be remembered, a centre-right demand resisted by the *left* as totalitarian!).

The third strand of a very traditional English and Scottish discourse about civil liberty quickly brings tensions both within and between political libertarian and neo-Burkean thought. Here we are concerned with the claim of many Whigs and Enlightenment figures that local self-government is – or at least can be – a central expression of political liberty. That tradition was never dominant in Britain, although its origins are deep in English history, but it has reached its fullest expression in the United States, which drew heavily on the Anglo-Scottish inheritance for the constitutional place of local government.[52] Political libertarians who regard the town hall as the most authoritarian and blunt element of the state have therefore been able to ally themselves with the neo-conservative current that has dominated the centre-right since the 1970s, which fears the capacity of local government to fetter the fiscal and policy autonomy of the centre. Indeed, it is but five or six years since a leading figure in the Major administration seriously canvassed the idea of abolishing local government in Britain altogether. That the idea was not pursued demonstrates not only political realism but also the continuing influence, however subaltern, of the neo-Burkean strain within the centre-right coalition.

Under Mr Hague, the Conservative Party has been faced with the urgent need to recruit and develop new political talent and has quietly begun to put party effort once again into local government. However, it has yet to show the kinds of policy interest in the vitality, let alone the fiscal autonomy of local government that might betoken an alliance between neo-Burkean ideas and a conception of political liberty more reminiscent of US neo-conservatism. It will be hard to do so after recently attacking the legitimacy of local government. Nevertheless, the time for such a political formation on the centre-right may have come. For the younger cohorts of people who are likely to be attracted to the centre-right in the next few years will to come to political maturity in a period when local government is at once more innovative and responsive than Whitehall and increasingly coming into conflict with the centralist strain in New Labour's thought.

One way that the centre-right can perhaps recover both the sources of political vitality and practical resources that are offered at the local level might be take up the new Labour challenge to innovate in the forms of local governance, and to welcome the possibility of local variation and more local *self*-government. Directly elected mayors, local cabinet structures, local referenda and perhaps even returning more power over local tax raising to the locality are all possibilities worth exploring. Not only would powerful local mayors offer neo-conservatives the chance once again to experiment with some statecraft, and neo-Burkeans the chance to explore new forms of plural authority, these innovations could offer neo-liberals and political libertarians the chance to show how their agenda for more personal liberty, lower taxes and greater use of market mechanisms could achieve popularity.

The ideal of political liberty may never play the crucial role in the ideas of the English centre-right that economic liberty does, or that it does in US neo-conservatism. But it will continue to be an important current of political sensibility and aspiration to which the centre-right will have to appeal, and with which the treaty with a re-imagined authority will have to make accommodations.

Neo-liberalism looking for the right partner

Despite the frequency with which people on the centre-left denounce Thatcherism as 'neo-liberalism', it should be clear by now that neo-liberalism was but one current in its settlement, and by no means the dominant one. Indeed, even in the supposed heartland of neo-liberalism in monetary policy, I have argued that the real appeal of monetarism to neo-conservatives was its ability to justify the taking of that field of policy making into the high politics of autonomous central state action guided only by rules, and as far as British politics can (lacking the means of constitutional entrenchment) away from the reach of interest group lobbying. In this sense, William Hague, Lord Parkinson and David Willetts have been right to stress that the perception that Conservative governments cared only for economics was quite wrong.

The basis of the treaty between neo-liberalism and neo-conservatism was twofold. At the intellectual level, it was based on the fact that economic liberty depends upon an agency with the authority to define and enforce property rights and, by corollary, to remove over-regulation and face down the restrictive practices that cramp economic liberty. At the more pragmatic level of low politics, neo-liberalism was an essential part of the claim of the Thatcherite settlement to articulate the interests of at least some significant seams of business in Britain.[53]

A valuable element of the next centre-right's inheritance from neo-liberalism is the sensibility that emphasises caution in policy making, because of the importance of unforeseeable and unintended consequences. Road transport policies that are based on projections of demand for cars and journeys have run into the unforeseen consequence that the number of journeys increased in response to the available road space; safety regulation has often had the unforeseen consequence that people using equipment built to new standards allow their own operating practices to be slapdash; many of the programmes of the welfare state have created poverty traps; and so on. As policy experts have offered up to politicians so many policies that have proven ineffective or even exacerbated the conditions they were meant to remedy, the public has understandably become less respectful of their authority. Any new centre-right political settlement, although it must nuance and qualify this impulse, will have to incorporate this recognition, not merely in the rhetoric of opposition to the inevitable unforeseen consequences of new Labour's activism, but within its own distinctive outlook.

Whatever else the next centre-right is or does, if it is to have a chance of securing power again it must re-engage with the challenge of articulating the interests of at least significant fractions of business. It must do so, moreover, in a situation in which, for the first time since the end of Lloyd George's long domination of British politics, it no longer has a monopoly of that role.

It is old news that business does not speak with one voice, save on some very fundamental issues of basic property rights. Differences between small and large, export-oriented and domestically-oriented, manufacturing and services, financial services and others are familiar parts of the business landscape. Even the principal umbrella bodies for business – Confederation of British Industry, Federation of Small Business and Institute of Directors – are but coalitions across these interests. And, of course, they rarely have good reasons for wanting to enter protracted and bitter conflict with any government of the day, unless it were to be of the hard left, which seems most unlikely. Individual neo-liberal commentators of the deepest dye protest their disdain for 'businessmen's economics' as semi-literate,[54] but neo-liberalising politicians cannot afford to stand quite so loftily above the fray of lobbying for political endorsement and patronage, government contracts, regulatory and fiscal favours and blatant rent-seeking which is the day-to-day stuff of the politics of individual businesses and industry associations. The neo-liberal agenda of deregulation of markets (save perhaps for competition law, where many who regard themselves as neo-liberals see a role for regulatory action), entrepreneurship, low taxation, secure property rights and economic liberty can appeal to a wide span of business interests, if not all.

There remain significant Poujadist pockets within the centre-right, articulating the short-term interests of small businesses in service industries serving customers directly rather than serving other, typically larger businesses. This group tends to be hostile the interests of big business, seeing it as somehow inherently corporatist and accommodating to over-regulation. To listen to these voices would be a mistake, and one that a dose of intelligent neo-liberalism can still correct. Not only does the centre-right need to appeal to big business in electoral and financial terms, there are important segments of small business in many regions of the country who cannot share this agenda. Moreover, the Poujadist view quickly allies itself not with deregulation but with a nationalism that would be damaging on other grounds.

But in the world that neo-conservatism and neo-liberalism helped to create, a growing number of the agencies that define and create guaranteed property rights, that determine the character of regulation and that create the basic order in markets on the basis of which investment decisions can be made and economic liberty grounded are international. The authority that neo-liberals need is no longer only that of the strong autonomous central state. And where the neo-liberal agenda does require the nation state to act, it requires ever greater coordination and syndication of powers with other nation states and with transnational bodies ranging from the International Standards Organisation and the World Trade Organisation to the European Union and other regional economic blocs. The basis of the alliance with neo-conservative commitment to the autonomy of the central state is steadily being eroded.

There are, of course, threats in the next decade to the achievements of internationalising neo-liberalism. Acute financial turmoil following the collapse of far eastern and Russian economies could conceivably lead to the rise of interest in protectionism in the mainstream of either or both leading parties in the US Congress. What has hitherto been the terrain of Ross Perot and Pat Buchanan could become centre-ground politics, if the US economy begins to turn sharply downward. It will be important for the centre-right in every country in the developed world to do what it can to head off a return of the combination of recession and protection that proved lethal in the inter-war years.

Both neo-liberal radicalism and a tradition of centre-right institutional design may yet come into their own in ways that are currently hard to foresee, because most of the system of transnational governance seems to neo-conservatives to be quintessentially both bureaucratic and weak. In a climate of still greater transnational business power and deepening interdependence of the global governance system, neo-liberalism may prove to be the great globalising ideology of the new informational capitalism. What the centre-right can bring to that party is its tradition – in part a gift from neo-Burkeans to help solve a problem set by neo-liberals – for messy, pragmatic, problem-solving institutional creativity. Unencumbered by the institutional tidy-mindedness of the left, the centre-right across the developed world has been able to develop a culture of political entrepreneurship in institutional creativity that has made important contributions to transnational governance. Untidy but effective arrangements such as the overlapping responsibilities of the Western European Union, NATO and the Organisation for Security and Cooperation in Europe owes much to the work of British conservative institutional work. The continental Christian democratic tradition has proven able to adapt both federal and centralist traditions at nation state level to solve problems at the continental level through a variety of institutions including the European Union, the Council of Europe, the Western European Union, the North Atlantic Treaty Organisation and the Organisation for Security Cooperation in Europe. Moreover, it has often been an important British centre-right contribution to make these arrangements work effectively. This alphabet soup of agencies frustrates the tidy-minded of both left and right, who see only bureaucratic muddle and inefficiency. Yet it has worked far better than anyone could have imagined in the 1940s and 1950s when the design process began. The network has not simply been a cat's cradle in which effective governance has been snared. Rather, it has managed with varying d delicacy, the extraordinary recovery of a continent from cat through huge ideological and territorial conflict prior to from ethnic war to secure tolerable absence of active war for much of the west and a rate of economic and trade growth that has delivered much that Europe's citizens have aspired to and much that many in Latin America, Asia and Africa still cannot.

The basic neo-liberal instinct in governance at any level is naturally and rightly impatient – secure property rights with the least cost and the most streamlined decision making and do nothing else! Unfortunately, property rights are not, in the real world of politics and business, secured with so little fuss. Institutional design must be messy; power and decision making must be shared, diffused and balanced in ways that, instinctively, neo-Burkeans have a better feel for than do neo-liberals.

Neo-liberalism alone, therefore, cannot be a viable centre-right project. Like political libertarianism, its tendency to alarm many, even among the better off, that they would remain without security and protection against risks were its ambitions fulfilled is not sustainable, nor is its ambition to take politics entirely out of economics. On the other hand, neo-liberalism is better fitted than neo-conservative or perhaps even the neo-Burkean sensibility to grapple effectively with the challenges of a world in which economic behaviour needs no borders and yet also calls for the buttressing of order and property.

Dangers of pessimism, currents of modernisation

The centre-right has, in the twentieth century, sometimes been associated with a pessimistic and Jeremiad critique of manners, morals and mores. Authoritarians often take original sin to be at the heart of law and order policy, and design policy accordingly around punishment. Similarly, the paleo-Burkean tradition has a deep suspicion of the optimism that is embedded in rationalistic projects for the amelioration of misery.[55] Some of the more arch on the right have sometimes suggested that poverty and misery for at least some are inevitable in human life and that it is both pointless and dangerous to attempt to alleviate them.

But not all the centre-right traditions share this pessimistic sensibility. The neo-liberal element in the Thatcherite settlement was deeply optimistic. Mrs Thatcher's own impatience with the idea of inevitable decline was directed as often against those on the right as upon the smug social democratic establishment. Moreover, in the economic aspirations of neo-liberalism is an optimistic belief that prosperity can be self-sustaining, even that wealth can 'trickle down' to the poorest. Optimism is the emotional politics of all radicalism, whether of the right or the left, and it characterised the centre-right radicalism of the 1980s as much it did the social democratic radicalism of the late 1940s.

Indeed, it can be argued that the centre-right has been most successful not merely in winning elections but in its more ambitious projects of influencing the shape and direction of cultural change in Britain, when it has been able to offer an optimistic vision of modernisation for the common life of the British people, its periods of least achievement have been those when it has offered 'safety first', business as usual and mere competent management of the inheritance. While the Thatcher years are the most recent example, they are by no means the only ones. For the foundation of the modern Conservative Party, we tend to look more to the moderniser Robert Peel, whose name is responsible for the modernisation of basic institutions such as the removal of outdated religious discrimination, and the instauration of modern policing. Disraeli modernised not only his own party but British democracy. Whatever one thinks of the record of the mercurial Joseph Chamberlain, his brief charisma was based less on personality than his ability to convince significant numbers at least for a while that tariff reform to buttress imperial preference represented the modernisation of the imperial legacy. The success years of MacMillan in the late 1950s were those when he was still able to encapsulate a sense of progress and advance. By contrast, the 'steady-as-she-goes' conservatism of Liverpool, Salisbury, almost any of the leaders of the 1920s and 1930s before Churchill, of the later MacMillan, Douglas Home, and the later period of John Major, has been conspicuously less successful, not only in electoral terms but in the building of a political project that could inspire and even understand, let alone work, with the nature of cultural change in Britain. The paleo-Burkean cry of 'change but only in order to conserve', which was far from Mrs Thatcher's credo, has merits as a useful reminder, a discipline against change for its own sake, against excesses and violations of worthwhile institutions and the authoritarianism that can be the handmaiden of radicalism. But when given the role of a strategic direction for the centre-right, it is quickly exhausted.

The next centre-right will have to recover some of that optimism about the possibilities that the twenty-first century will bring. The fashionable pessimism of the authoritarian right about an impending 'clash of civilisations', or of the paleo-Burkean cultural critics about the vulgarisation of the arts and media, will serve the centre-right ill. To be sure, in the next few years, the fall out from the east Asian and Russian crises and the impact of speculation against the euro on the money markets will create financial instability, and there remain major political risks in Russia, central Africa, Central Asia, Korea, Cuba and the Middle East. But short and even medium term threats are always with us. The key issue is not the scale of world disorder but the scope of possibilities the new century brings for prosperity, peace and innovation: it is these aspirations that the next centre-right must articulate and express powerfully.

The centre-right will find the sources and reasons for that optimism more readily and more abundantly in the neo-liberal tradition than in almost any other centre-right tradition, for neo-liberalism can offer solid evidence from the best experiences of the twentieth century about what capitalism can bring in enrichment, liberty and opportunity and the solution of social and even environmental problems.

The interesting question for the centre-right is not whether rationalism is optimistic – the answer is surely yes – but whether all optimism is necessarily rationalistic in the naïve and dangerous sense that neo-Burkean sensibilities fear, namely that it will be reckless of unintended consequences and ride roughshod over the fabric of vibrant social and cultural life and over the plural sources of authority.[56] The centre-right has in the past been able to construct settlements of its political cultures in which optimistic and reforming projects could be conceived and for which a forward-looking public inspiration could be marshalled, without being guilty of the sins to which the neo-Burkeans point. Perhaps the 1980s were not such a period, as Ferdinand Mount and Simon Jenkins argue.[57] On the other hand, there are nineteenth century British models in the projects of Disraeli and Peel, and there are examples of optimistic centre-right projects for modernisation in continental Europe such as Adenauer's ambitions for Germany in the late 1940s and 1950s, on which the next centre-right will be able to draw.

'Modernisation' is a word that many will want to resist. Indeed, the description of the ambitions of Mrs Thatcher as 'modernising' is not one that she herself regularly used. Even among those who would not convict modernisers of all the sins which naïve rationalism is heir to, there is made a respectable argument that modernisation is a phenomenon, like happiness and love but unlike material success and the remedy of specific evils, that cannot be aimed at directly, but can only be the side-effect of other programmes. There is something to this argument, at least when couched in Burkean terms of the dangers that excessive attachment to abstractions and universal claims in politics can lead to. On the other hand, what remains so impressive about the achievements of Peel, Disraeli and Thatcher is precisely the national and local particularism of their conception of modernisation and of their optimism and the fact that, while each policy initiative was certainly not geared to a grand abstract vision, without that vision neither the electoral success nor the motivation for the concrete achievements would have been possible.

The international traditions

This is not the place to assess the future of US neo-conservatism in its American heartlands or the prospects for Christian democracy or Gaullism in their specific European settings. The important question here is to consider how their legacy might affect the next settlement of the centre-right within the British isles – which is, admittedly, difficult to answer without more information about their prospects in their domestic bases.

The principal and distinctive contribution of US neo-conservatism to centre-right debates in Britain has not been its emphasis on familial authority, revealed religion or presidential autonomy in Machiavellian foreign policy. Rather, its special contribution flows from its peculiarly American context of devolved federalism. Where neo-Burkeans see decentralised and plural institutions in governance and civil society operating in a fluid and evolving legal setting, in which common law and the vagaries of current legislation provide the background, US neo-conservatives stress the importance of the constitutionally entrenched guarantee of autonomy and self-government for local communities. US neo-conservatism resembles Paine's constitutional decentralisation more than Burke's vision of a decentralised world of the common law and custom and practice. It is this devolution of power from the central state, especially in any guaranteed form, which has proven even more difficult for British neo-conservatives to accept than neo-Burkean ambitions for diffused sovereignty.

In the British context, then, the key question is whether the constitutional changes that will be inherited by the next centre-right from New Labour will effectively force the centre-right down the road of some kind of constitutionally guaranteed subsidiarity, albeit – except in an independent Scotland if there were to be one by then – presumably without the facility of constitutional entrenchment. The main New Labour proposals on the horizon today that might suggest that this is possible are those which may one day permit regional assemblies, the new directly elected London mayor and strategic authority and the possibility of directly elected mayors in other cities, and the vaguer hints of greater fiscal powers for at least some local authorities. At the time of writing, it is hard to imagine that they would force a future centre-right government in England to accept a US-style constitutional status for local government however quickly implemented and however irreversible such arrangements might be. Indeed, the sheer size of the US almost insists upon a different model of governance from that in the tightly knit and tiny British Isles.

However, it is conceivable that the next centre-right might actually want to think about the merits of such arrangements. Neo-liberals have, after all, long argued that one of the merits of a constitutional basis for local government might be that local governments could be allowed to go bankrupt without any need for the central state to bail them out. Even neo-conservatives have sometimes felt the power of the argument that constitutionally independent local government would leave the centre free from blame when things go wrong locally, and would avoid the centre getting tangled up in responsibility for local budget-setting and taking the resulting unpopularity. The merit of the constitutional separation is that, if it is complete, the traditional economic concerns about the impact of high taxing and spending local governments upon the central fisc are dealt with at a stroke. Moreover, it would provide a useful way of meeting the demand for more political participation without endangering other centre-right commitments to authority.

In the context of an independent Scotland, of course, it is much harder to know what the merits of a constitutional separation between Edinburgh and the town hall might be, but it is certainly possible to imagine highly centralising coalitions involving Scots nationalists in the early years of such an independent Scotland, to which constitutional separation might prove an attractive and popular centre-right response.

The inheritance and the challenge

From this audit of the resources that the next centre-right will inherit from the last, then, I conclude that each of the traditions bequeaths something of value, but must surrender something or at least accept that one of its aspirations must be counter-balanced. Figure 2 summarises the argument so far.

If this argument is accepted, then it suggests that the next centre-right settlement will represent a major rebalancing of the key traditions, by contrast with that of the Thatcher and Major years. In particular, this suggests that, whereas the settlement that lasted from the mid-1970s to the mid-1990s was one in which the centre of gravity of the centre-right was in neo-conservatism, with neo-liberalism and neo-Burkeanism as subaltern elements, the heart of a viable new settlement could be between neo-Burkeanism and neo-liberalism. In this case, the settlement would, as I suggested at the beginning of this book, represent a genuinely and distinctively centre-right settlement which is not principally conservative.

In the terms set out in the opening section, the implication of this argument for the nature of the re-thinking of the idea of authority is that

- *macro-social authority* will likely consist of a network of tiers and institutions at the local, national, regional and transnational levels, none of which will have autonomy from one another: while the task for this authority will be buttressing of property rights internationally and the disciplining of special interests, cartels and other threats to economic liberty, it will also be to sustain the

Figure 2. The legacy inherited by the next centre-right			
Tradition	Positive resources worth building on	Currents that require counter-balancing	Major problems
Neo-conservatism	The state is inevitably an enterprise association A viable conception of authority is needed in any society, and must include both macro-social and micro-social elements	Tendency to authoritarianism	The autonomous central state committed to high politics is of declining usefulness in an age of interdependent tiers of governance Household forms are changing: women's participation in the labour force is irre-versible and makes certain traditional ideas about micro-social authority unviable
Neo-Burkeanism	Recognition of plurality of sources of authority Recognition of the criti-cal role of the local Messy institutional creativity Articulation of environ-mental concern and risk prevention	Tendency to romanticise and protect beyond their usefulness existing authori-tative institutions	Paleo-Burkean ideal that eternal incremental change in ancient insti-tutions will produce socially optimal systems is no longer culturally acceptable
Political libertarianism	Importance of political liberty Recognition of the role of the local Recognition of civil liberties	Individualisation of authority	Basic ideal is culturally unviable: permitting participation but consti-tutionally debarring it from having effect is not acceptable; there are limits to the extent that even middle class people will accept the individu-alisation of risk
Neo-liberalism	Economic liberty Optimism and commit-ment to modernisation Caution about unin-tended consequences Recognition of the central fact that transna-tionalisation of economic life makes autonomous economic regulatory jurisdiction unviable Capacity to articulate some key interests of significant currents within business	Impatience and excessive tidy-mindedness in institutional design	There are limits even to middle class willingness to accept individualisa-tion of risk Politics cannot be removed wholly from economics

institutional, organisational, social and cultural basis on which individualism and liberty are possible; and that

- *micro-social authority* will take diverse forms, including but not restricted to parental authority over children, but also greater roles for local governance institutions, perhaps even with some kind of constitutional separation from national government.

Furthermore, the new treaty between the impulses to liberty and to authority would, on this argument, be shaped by a recognition of the importance of political participation and civil liberties.

In the introduction, I claimed that this argument would offer an outline sketch of something genuinely centre-right (although my personal politics are of the radical centre) and not simply a disguised version of a radical centre programme. This claim can now be tested.

There are, in my view, clear and distinctly centre-right features of this settlement that would not be expected to appear in a programme of the radical centre. Firstly and most centrally, the abiding commitment of the centre-right to articulate and develop the role of authority is placed firmly at the heart of the agenda. Secondly, economic liberty and the neo-liberal agenda of market deregulation – with the clear acceptance that business power has a vital place in the modern world – are unambiguously to the fore. By contrast, a radical centre would place much less emphasis on the blunt importance of authority – without, of course, falling into the infantile romanticism of the egalitarian left that all authority is authoritarian – and would nuance the neo-liberal agenda the recognition that markets are rooted in social structure and in culture, and that business power sometimes needs to be shaped with institutions that can nurture – or revolutionise – social structure and culture in more viable directions.

On the other hand, it is worth asking the converse question. In the not-too-distant past, there were tactical alliances between the radical centre and the centre-right, to oppose the overweening power of the trades unions and the professions, to open up markets from restrictive practices and to meritocracy, and – more recently – with some neo-Burkean elements of the centre-right to make the case for plural sources of authority. One measure of how great the change would be if the next centre-right settlement looked anything like that set out here would be to ask whether such tactical alliances between radical centre and centre-right could be revived, if there were dangers posed by the centre-left that also concerned those of the radical centre – perhaps some renascent Fabian statism, or punitive income taxation, an attempt to impose unviable regulation of transnational capital flows, a revival of the 'closed shop', or a regime of corporate governance that would make effective decision making impossible. Naturally, one hopes that the centre-left will not again resort to such backward-looking policies, and to be fair, at present, they are thankfully not on the horizon. On the other hand, as the distinctiveness of the radical centre agenda develops, it is quite possible that at some stage, today's uneasy tactical alliance with the centre-left may break down. My own view is that short-term tactical alliances between this kind of new centre-right and the radical centre might again be conceivable. If, of course, the centre-right wanted them.

Authority and risk: from settlement to policy

If this argument about the basic settlement that could underpin the next centre-right is broadly right, then we can begin to see some of the outlines of the policy stances that will be at its heart.

Public policy is in the first place about how risks are to be managed – responding to the negative is the first step, before promoting the positive. So, for example, economic policy is concerned with how risks such as economic shocks can be anticipated or, failing that, coped with; how damage to productivity and competitiveness can be averted or at least contained; how risks of inflation, unemployment, slump and other evils can be prevented or at least controlled. Social (and for that matter environmental) policy is concerned with the balance of responsibility between taxpayers on the one hand and individuals, households and private associations and firms on the other in addressing risks that individuals, households, associations and firms face, and, where the taxpayer must accept some responsibility, with the appropriate strategies for addressing such risks – providing insurance for the costs of cure or palliation, and/or putting in place some form of prevention. Likewise, defence policy is concerned with risks to military and territorial security.

In this section, I will argue that the prospects for preventing harms will be central both to the reinvention of the centre-right after the 1997 electoral defeats in Britain and the 1995-96 defeats in the USA, as well as the debate about how the centre-left is to re-create itself, currently being conducted under the rubric of 'the third way'. I begin with an exploration the nature of risk prevention, and then move on to situate arguments about the proper scope and balance of responsibility for prevention within the prospects for a new settlement within the centre-right.

Preventive action is usually divided into three levels of activity:

- *Primary prevention* – preventing harms from befalling people in the first place
- *Secondary prevention* – postponing the time when harms will set in
- *Tertiary prevention* – preventing harms that have occurred from getting worse or from recurring.

Moreover, prevention may be targeted at

- the whole population or large sub-groups, the environment, situations
- those individuals most at risk
- those individuals to whom harms have already occurred.

This yields the classification set out in Figure 3 opposite (examples of the types of activity are given in each cell).

While whole population, environmental and situational prevention is most commonly primary, and prevention targeted upon those to whom harms have occurred is by definition tertiary, in practice, at risk group and population, situation and environmental strategies can be used at all three levels.

A set of ideas about how a society ought to be governed that amounts to a model of political economy (or even, which is less demanding, an ideology)[58] will centrally concern itself with how the risks that individuals and groups face should be addressed. Free market liberals confine the list of risks for the costs of curing or palliating harms that they would have taxpayers socially insure citizens – typically, being attacked by military forces from foreign states, being a victim of crime, being the subject of lesser harms from others, having contracts dishonoured, and so on. Social democrats believed that taxpayers should as far as possible socially insure citizens against the costs of providing curative or at least palliative services after the fact of harm in the case of at least some additional risks – typically, ill-

Figure 3: Types of prevention – some examples

Target: Strategy:	Populations, groups, environment, situations	People most at risk	People who have suffered harms
Primary – *prevention of* *onset or occur-* *rence*	Fluoridation of drinking water	Selective vaccination of elderly people against specific flu strains Diversion programmes for adolescents at risk of becoming delinquent	n/a
Secondary – *postponement*	Subsidy for facilities providing activities for retired people Situational crime prevention activity	Diet and exercise counselling for those with high blood pressure or high blood cholesterol levels	n/a
Tertiary – *prevention of* *worsening or* *recurrence*	Clear-up of oil spills	n/a	Conventional medical treatment Probation work with offenders

health and disability, frailty in old age, unemployment and inadequate basic education.

One way to think about politics, then, is to classify ideologies and models of political economy according to the ways they answer the questions,

1. For which risks should individuals, households or private organisations should take responsibility, and for which should taxpayers shoulder responsibility collectively?
2. Where the taxpayer is deemed to have some responsibility for a risk, in which cases is the most appropriate response one of intervention after the fact of harm (cure, palliation) and in which is it most appropriate principally or even only to intervene before (prevention)? (Of course, some risks may call for effort supported by taxpayers in both strategies.)

3. If it considered that the taxpayer should have some responsibility for addressing the risks of ill-health and disability, unemployment and inadequate basic education, then how far should risk management observe the principle which is accepted by almost all in security, law and property rights, that social protection should be no respecter of persons but should provide a standard service, and, conversely, how far should a more personalised, particular (preventive or curative) service be provided to meet individual, household, locality or social group preferences or needs?

This way of thinking about politics yields the general classification of centre-right and centre-left ideologies as set out in Figure 4 opposite.

Ideologies are not found embodied in pure form in any particular country – practical politics requires too many compromises to build winning coalitions for that. But one can readily identify dominant strains, coalitions between forces adopting these risk ideologies and trends over time from one to another. So, in Britain, if the 1945 Labour government set in place a social democratic risk politics, the Conservative administrations of the 1979-1997 period, for all their liberal rhetoric, succeeded in practice only in shifting, depending on the particular field of public policy, toward preventive liberalism (for example, encouraging people to take out private pensions and gradually allowing inflation to erode the real value of the state pension and phasing out the state earnings related pension) or only to preventive social democracy (such as the *Health of the nation* commitments to preventive public health medicine).

In Britain today, as in some other developed countries, there is, whether or not one welcomes the fact, declining popular and élite interest in the positions of undiluted liberalism and of social democracy. A majority of citizens does not appear to have been convinced by the liberal arguments about the merits of taking more personal, family or private responsibility and, as a corollary, having more freedom, as successive studies of public attitudes and political culture have shown. On the other hand, social democracy has fallen out of favour, not so much because a majority of the people have grown to dislike the *scope* of its protections against risk (although some do), but

Figure 4. Ideologies and risk

Taypayer responsible for:	Curative provision of security, enforcement of basic civil and criminal law and property rights only	Primary prevention, but not social insurance against costs of cure or provision of cure for sickness, disability, frailty, unemployment, inadequate (generally only basic) education	Both cure and prevention of sickness, disability, frailty, unemployment; Provision of (at least basic) education	Cure and palliation of sickness, disability, frailty, unemployment; Provision of (at least basic) education
Ideology / political economy	Liberalism	Preventive liberalism	Preventive social democracy	Social democracy
Service model	Standard service	Typically standardised model of service (regulation, incentive, etc), but some personalisation	Standard or personalised	Standard service

the *model* of the service it offers. Thus, parents who can afford it choose private schools where their children may receive more individual tuition, households choose private medical care for more choice of remedies than those available within the rationed public system, and so on.

If this broad description of recent and current trends in political risk culture in Britain and some similar countries is accurate, then the challenge for the next few years for both the centre-left and the centre-right is to think through not only the *range* of risks for which they want to socialise responsibility for, but also how far they *want* to and they *can* shift within the space of preventive liberalism and preventive social democracy, toward more prevention and more personalisation of socialised risk management.

The political resources within the centre-right are divided in their answers to the central questions of the scope of prevention. Strict neo-liberals have tended to stress the dangers of prevention, on the grounds that the inherently unforeseeable and unintended consequences of preventive action can be significant and costly, save in the field of military defence where there is no alternative to an anticipatory stance. Pure liberals from John Stuart Mill onward have sometimes been suspicious of commitments to preventive efforts financed by the taxpayer. The cultural bias of liberalism has been to stress the unpredictability of the future and hence the futility of much of the anticipatory effort on which preventive public policy rests.

On the questions of responsibility for handling risks, traditionally, liberal and neo-liberal perspectives on the management of risk have been to emphasise the responsibility of individuals, households, private associations and firms for addressing the risks of unemployment, sickness and ill-health, poor educational attainment and many kinds of environmental damage, but to accept as the taxpayers' responsibility the financing of largely curative responses to crime and other threats to law and order, with only a very limited preventive role in macroeconomic management. The liberal suspicion has been that a commitment to prevention financed by taxpayers risks not merely ineffectiveness, irrelevance and waste – social policy Maginot lines – the erosion of individual or household responsibility. Rather, to cope with economic shocks and emergencies, liberals have preferred to see the public finances run small but sufficient surpluses to respond resiliently and flexibly with curative action after the event of harm, rather than acting preventatively. Private responsibility and a commitment to cure have run hand in hand in the liberal sensibility. In liberal thought, then, the constitutional restrictions upon the scope of the authority of public power are intimately connected with its belief that risk is inevitable, that risk-taking is desirable, that people should be expected and encouraged to bear risks and that protection and prevention of risk corrupt.

The neo-Burkean current of thought is less rigid both in the constraints it would place upon the responsibility of the taxpayer and in the kinds of strategies that it would consider appropriate. On the other hand, Neo-Burkeans have tended to see a greater role for collective support for prevention of at least a restricted set of harms, where individuals cannot reasonably expect to take effective action themselves, while recognising that the scope for effective action widens as new individual technologies emerge (burglar alarms, self-health methods, household waste recycling) and contract as the nature of some problems become more transnational. While preferring individual or associational means for handling risk, it is as interested in vertical subsidiarity within the public institutions of governance as in the horizontal subsidiarity that devolves responsibility from the state to individuals, households, private associations and firms. There is in the neo-Burkean strain a recognition of the role that local institutions of governance can play in managing risks, as well as a commitment (that liberals sometimes disdain) to the idea that people want and need a measure of security and protection against risk and uncertainty, and that they reasonably look to the institutions of governance for this. Indeed, the paleo-Burkean commitment to the preservation of ancient institutions is itself a manifestation of that sensibility which sees continuity as an important element in the role of authority in providing bulwarks against uncertainty and risk. Contrary to the liberal connection between risk and authority, the neo-Burkean current regards the diffusion of authority as a key element in the management of risk, and is prepared to contemplate some socialisation of risk, while still securing the economic predominance of private property and a predominantly capitalist economy.

Does this contrast then undermine my argument that there can be a new settlement between these two currents? I believe not, although of course it shows the breadth of the gap to be bridged by a new and viable centre-right. Practical politics is not built upon the simplicities of ideological consistency, but on the more complex and messy pursuit of the culturally viable. My argument is that the neo-liberal and the neo-Burkean strains are, for all their contrasts and whatever their popular or intellectual limitations, being thrown together as the principal resources culturally available to the centre-right; it will be the practical task of the next generation of centre-right politicians to make them work together for a period that might last as long as a generation. The resulting marriage of Burke and Smith will be no more intellectually pure than was Thatcherism, but it may stand some chance of challenging the still broader and, in the medium term, no doubt culturally endangered centre-left coalition.

The advantage of a settlement between neo-Burkean and neo-liberal political sensibilities is that while neo-liberalism can support and put public value upon entrepreneurial risk-taking, people will only accept this if they feel protected from risks in other areas of life, and the neo-Burkean current may be able to offer that countervailing balance. Those who see global economic interdependence as an opportunity also tend to see the same phenomenon as one that makes for intolerable insecurity, at least during the troughs of the business cycle.

For the present purpose, the details of the economic and social policies put forward by a future centre-right coalition between neo-liberals and neo-Burkeans are less important than the principles that would inform them. The arguments offered here about authority and risk suggest the following could be principles for economic and social policy around which such a coalition might be able to unite.

Recognising that the boundaries of the nation state are no longer the ones by which risk can be managed, the next centre-right should focus much of its effort on the syndication of the management of risk between countries and trading blocs in the major economic regions of the world.

The simple neo-liberal ambition for the privatisation of risk management and the scaling back of the welfare state should be tempered with the neo-Burkean concern for the importance of the popular sense of security against economic turbulence and the ineluctable risks of human life. Abandoning the overriding neo-conservative concern for the autonomy of the central state that resulted in over-centralisation of the management of risk, the next centre-right would tolerate much greater local and regional variety in the ways in which risk is managed, while positively encouraging the networking of local and regional strategies with international ones without necessarily having first to pass through the licensing of Whitehall – or, for that matter, Edinburgh in an independent Scotland. The local particularism to which neo-Burkeans cleave can be made to fit well with the neo-liberal suspicion of one-size-fits-all standardisation in the services in which there remains a public interest.

Moreover, the next centre-right might be able to strike a quite different balance between the size of the taxpayers' burden and the strategies for the management of risk than liberals have wanted to, or than previous centre-right coalitions have felt able to. For there are some preventive strategies to deal with sickness, accidents, crime and environmental damage that, if better developed, could reduce the size of the bills for curative interventions of medicine, detective policing and environmental clean-up, in ways that should reassure neo-liberals. While some curative bills can only be postponed – if we live long enough, we all die of some degenerative disease – secondary prevention strategies can reduce the length of time that curative work is needed. For example, it is now possible, by preventive means, to shorten the necessary period of frailty and need for long term care at the end of life. Too often in the recent past, curative medicine has been used to prolong the quantity of life even at the expense of protracted pain, indignity and sickness.

For a centre-right anxious to shake off the public image of being concerned solely with economic policy and interests and willing to accept that citizens will continue to demand some measure of collective protection against risk, but also capable of recognising that autonomous nation states and any single family form will no longer sustain authority, the neo-liberal strain needs a partnership with the neo-Burkean.

Conclusion

There is little that is inevitable about politics, and certainly it is not foreordained that the next centre-right will take the shape I have outlined here.

On the other hand, when major currents of political sensibility look backward to lost golden ages, when they refuse to accept the unviability of the particular settlements they were attached to in the recent past, they risk becoming – or remaining – marginalised. The centre-right in Britain is in disarray, and it will need to re-think its positions fundamentally if it is once again to construct the kind of project that could govern, at least at the central level in England, with the kind of hegemonic ambition that characterised it for much of the twentieth century.

The revival of the centre-left and its current, if not altogether happy, tactical alliance with the radical centre, presents a major challenge of a kind that the centre-right has not had to face since Gladstone or Lloyd George. Yet the centre-right has regrouped and shifted its ground fundamentally after each electoral disaster and major dislocation from the centre of gravity in British political culture. After the utter rout of 1906, it took Conservatism ten years to find a coherent and positive response of its own to the situation inherited from the New Liberalism and the war. After the Labour government elected in 1945 drastically reshaped the landscape of British institutions and political culture, Conservatism repositioned itself, not merely by accepting the irreversible, but by trying to rebalance its own traditions to find a positive and distinctive way forward under Churchill and MacMillan. After the debacle of 1964, the process that led to Selsdon in 1970 represented a new way of making a settlement between liberty and authority, and after the ignominious collapse of 1974, the Thatcherite project gradually took shape. The task today is of the same order – not merely in the gradient of the psephological cliff-face to be climbed, but in the scale of the intellectual problem presented for a coherent centre-right outlook for whatever will be the governance arrangements of the British Isles in the information age.

The prospect of a centre-right settlement in the British Isles that is not conservative will seem strange to many readers, for whom centre-right and conservative are synonyms, or who prefer, by definitional fiat, to claim for neo-conservatism the other traditions that I have distinguished from it. If my argument about the depth of the crisis facing the neo-conservative conception of authority is accepted, then it matters very much that we all – whatever our politics – begin to think through the implications for the centre-right. Getting the terms straight is an important first step.

There will almost certainly be a revival in the political and cultural fortunes of the centre-right in the next decade. Whether that revival offers the prospect of power, whether it offers a viable and sustainable settlement between the impulses to liberty and authority matters enormously, and not only to those on centre-right. The best chance of achieving that is to begin to imagine how these abiding commitments will look when their connection with neo-conservatism has been broken. That will come hard to many traditionalists. But the centre-right has always been at its most successful when it has demonstrated a compelling agenda for modernisation of life in Britain – a terrain currently claimed by the centre-left. The best hope for the centre-right project of modernity in the twenty-first century, therefore, is a quite new cultural settlement between authority and liberty. How long such a settlement lasts will depend not only upon events but upon the skills with which the centre-right reassembles itself. It is quite possible that, with care and a little luck, the settlement that the next British centre-right builds may lead the centre-right of much of the developed world in the new century.

Notes

1. Muller JZ, 1997, 'What is conservative social and political thought?' in Muller JZ, ed, *Conservatism an anthology of social and political thought from David Hume to the present*, Princeton University press, Princeton New Jersey, 3-31; Willetts D, 1992, *Modern conservatism*, Penguin, Harmondsworth; Scruton R, 1980, *The meaning of conservatism*, Penguin, Harmondsworth; Devigne R, 1994, *Recasting conservatism: Oakeshott, Strauss and the response to postmodernism*, Yale, University Press, New Haven.
2. Malcolm N, 1996, 'Conservatism realism and Christian democracy', in Minogue K, ed, *Conservative realism: new essays in conservatism*, HarperCollins, London, 44-67.
3. Whiteley P, Seyd P and Richardson J, 1994, *True blues: the politics of Conservative Party membership*, Oxford University Press, Oxford.
4. Seldon A, 1996, *How Tory governments fall: the Tory party in power since 1783*, HarperCollins, London.
5. Gray J, 1995, *The undoing of Conservatism*, Social Market Foundation, London, reprinted with a new epilogue in Gray J and Willetts D, 1997, *Is Conservatism dead?*, Social Market Foundation, London.
6. Such as the historian of the Conservative Party, Lord Blake (many broadcast appearances, 1997-98), or the conservative political scientist James Bulpitt and the many who follow him: Bulpitt J, 1985, 'The discipline of the new democracy: Mrs Thatcher's domestic statecraft', *Political Studies*, vol 34, no 1, 19-39: see discussion in Marquand D, 1992, 'The enterprise culture: old wine in new bottles', in Heelas P and Morris P, eds, *The values of the enterprise culture*, Routledge, London, 61-72.
7. I draw here heavily upon the cultural theory of the great British anthropologist, Mary Douglas and the late great American political scientist, Aaron Wildavsky, as developed by their students and many others. See Douglas M, 1978, *Cultural bias*, Royal Anthropological Institute, London; Douglas M and Wildavsky A, 1983, *Risk and danger: an essay on the selection of technological and environmental dangers*, University of California Press, Berkeley; Douglas M, 1994, *Risk and blame: essays in cultural theory*, Routledge, London; Douglas M, 1996, *Thought styles*, Sage, London; Thompson

M, Ellis R and Wildavsky A, 1990, *Cultural theory*, Westview, Boulder, Colorado; Coyle D and Ellis R, eds, 1994, *Politics, policy and culture*, Westview Press, Boulder, Colorado; Ellis R and Thompson M, eds, 1997, *Culture matters: essays in honour of Aaron Wildavsky*, Westview press, Boulder, Colorado; Adams J, 1995, *Risk*, UCL Press, London; 6 P, 1998, *The future of privacy, volume 1: private life and public policy*, Demos, London; 6 P, 1998, 'Housing policy in the risk archipelago: toward anticipatory and holistic government', *Housing Studies*, vol 13, no 3, 347-376.

Figure i summarises the understanding of political cultures which I draw from this tradition.

Figure i. Principal types of political culture			
grid ▲	▲ *Social relations are conceived as If they were principally involuntary* ▲		
	Fatalism *Systems are capricious*	*Hierarchy* *Systems are necessary*	
Individual ◄ *autonomy should not always be held accountable*	Systems deliver luck and misery arbitrarily; property owners can usually expect unfettered rights: my participation would be pointless. Tends to passivity.	Systems must be maintained in orderly state of balance by rational management, allowing appropriate roles for all positions to maintain balance of risk and opportunity. Private life must be cultivated but channelled. Tends to brittleness from excessive control	► *Individual autonomy should be accountable*
	Individualism *Regulated systems are superfluous or harmful*	*Egalitarianism* *Systems are oppressive except when they protect*	
	Benign, effective social systems are the product of the natural and spontaneous coordination of individual decisions. Constraining those decisions with regulated social systems will reduce supply and make everyone worse off in the long run; property rights should generally be protected. Exit can be substituted for voice. Tends to weak organisation.	Egalitarian social systems must be protected. Other social systems are oppressive and should be regulated and designed to prevent worst risks and distribute costs of protection fairly across society: solidarity within communities and by the rich to the poor is important. High levels of active participation are believed to be sustainable. Private life is suspect. Tends to fission and schism	
	▼ *Social relations are conceived as if they were principally voluntary* ▼		► group

The basic dimensions of any political culture are those which indicate the extent to which people are seen as basically accountable to a social group for their actions and even beliefs ('group'), and the extent to which the relations between people are seen as basically voluntary or involuntary and, correlatively the extent to which society is seen as fundamentally a matter of rules ('grid'). Cross-tabulating the two dimensions and distinguishing high and low grid and group yields four basic impulses of political culture that well up in any society. High group, high grid yields hierarchy or the impulse to authority and the belief that risk must be managed. Diagonally opposite lies the low group, low grid culture of individualism, associated with the impulse to liberty and an optimistic faith that risks can and should be borne individually and will on the average yield advantage and improvement. High grid, low group cultures exhibit despotism at the top of society and fatalism at the bottom. Fatalism shows up in two ways. Among élites, it is associated with grand pessimism about human nature and a deep rejection of meliorism about society, and among the subaltern groups, it is associated with civic privatism, quietism and, in more traditional societies than this, with learned deference. In both cases, risks are seen as something inevitable, about which politics can do little. Egalitarians, always prone to the creation of bohemian enclaves and schism, are committed to the idea that people should be protected from risk by collective institutions.

Any sophisticated and durable political tradition must make settlements between these basic biases – and make them afresh as they come apart in every generation due to the tensions that erupt in crises between these basic cultural impulses. Figures ii, iii, iv and v show in very general terms the territory on Figure i over which the main political traditions in Britain have sought to make settlements.

Figure ii. Typical neo-Conservative / neo-liberal settlements 1975-1997

Fatalism	Hierarchy
Individualism	Egalitarianism

Figure iii. Typical authoritarian 'Peterhouse' / Spectator settlements

Fatalism	Hierarchy
Individualism	Egalitarianism

Figure iv. Typical socialist settlements

Fatalism	Hierarchy
Individualism	Egalitarianism

Figure v. The ambition of the Blairites for a 'third way' settlement

Fatalism	Hierarchy
Individualism	Egalitarianism

8. Turnbull C, 1973, *The Ik*, Methuen, London.

9. Cowling M, 1997, *A conservative future*, Politeia, London.

10. Scruton, 1980 (note 1).

11. Gamble A, 1990, *The free market and the strong state*, Macmillan, Basingstoke.

12. Oakeshott M, 1951, 'Political education', in Laslett P, ed, 1970, *Philosophy, politics and society*, first series, Basil Blackwell, Oxford, 1-21; Oakeshott M, 1960, *Rationalism in politics and other essays*, Methuen, London; Oakeshott M, 1933, *Experience and its modes*, Cambridge University Press, Cambridge; Oakeshott M, 1975, *On human conduct*, Oxford University Press, Oxford; see also Devigne, 1994 (note 1) and Grant R, 1990, *Thinkers of our time: Oakeshott*, Claridge, London.

13. Willetts, 1992 (note 1); Willetts D, 1994, *Civic conservatism*, Social Market Foundation, London, reprinted with a new epilogue in Gray and Willetts, 1997 (note 5).

14. Mount F, 1992, *The British constitution now*, Mandarin, London.

15. Jenkins S, 1995, *Accountable to none: the Tory nationalisation of Britain*, Penguin, Harmondsworth.

16. Especially Scruton, 1980 (note 1); see also Scruton R, ed, 1991, *Conservative texts: an anthology*, Macmillan, Basingstoke.

17. Gray, 1995 (note 5); Gray J, 1993, *Beyond the new right*, Routledge, London; Gray J, 1996, *After social democracy*, Demos, London.

18. Kristol I, 1996, 'America's "exceptional conservatism"', in Minogue, 1996 (note 2).

19. Bell D, 1996, *The cultural contradictions of capitalism*, twentieth anniversary edition, Basic Books, New York.

20. I have drawn here on the valuable comparison between British and American neo-conservatisms by Robert Devigne, 1995, *Recasting conservatism: Oakeshott, Strauss and the response to postmodernism*, Yale University Press, New Haven.

21. Patten C, 1991, 'The power to change' (interview with David Marquand), *Marxism Today*, February, 20-23.

22. Malcolm, 1996 (note 2), 44-67.

23. Evans R, 1996, 'Whose is this image and superscription? Money and sovereignty', in Minogue, 1996 (note 2), 112-128.

24. Mount, 1992 (note 14).

25. Cooper R, 1996, *The postmodern state and the world order*, Demos, London.

26. I am grateful to Tim Hames for allowing me the use of this phrase.

27. In Oakeshott's terms, by being a 'civil association' nor an 'enterprise association': Oakeshott, 1960 (note 12); Oakeshott, 1975 (note 12); see also Devigne, 1994 (note 1) and Grant, 1990 (note 12).

28. 6 P, 1997, *Holistic government*, Demos, London: For evidence that these are the principal priorities of the public, see MORI, monthly, *British public opinion*, MORI, London.

29. As Lord Dahrendorf has repeatedly warned in Germany and in east central Europe since the fall of communism (Dahrendorf R, 1997, *After 1989: morals, revolution and civil society*, Macmillan, Basingstoke) and as Oakeshott warned in Britain: see Grant, 1990 (note 12).

30. Devigne, 1994 (note 1), 182-83, describing views of Glazer, Kirkpatrick and Podhoretz.

31. Strictly, of course, any power capable of ensuring social order can manage risk and hold chaos at bay. By authority, most people understand 'legitimate authority', or the deliberate exercise power where that power is subject both to social norms (Wrong DH, 199, *Power: its forms, bases and uses*, Transaction books, New York, 49-52) and to accepted systems of appointment and accountability (McMahon C, 1994, *Authority and democracy: a general theory of government and management*, Princeton University press, Princeton, New Jersey, esp ch 2. See also Raz J, 1986, *The morality of freedom*, Oxford University Press, Oxford, ch 4)

32. The locus classicus is of course, the overly famous description of the state of nature as one of war in Hobbes Leviathan: 'and the life of man, solitary, poor, nasty, brutish and short'. (Hobbes T, [1651] 1968, *Leviathan, or the matter, form and power of a commonwealth ecclesiastical and civil*, Penguin, Harmondsworth, 186.) Burke's view of the disorders in revolutionary France in the Reflections is a constant reference point for Conservatives when considering the dangers of the disruption of legitimate authority., while Matthew Arnold's thoughts on mob violence in Culture and anarchy are today less frequently recalled. That the undermining of authority can damage cultures of morality and duty is a central theme in Irving Kristol's well-known essay, 'Pornography, obscenity and the case for censorship' (excerpted in Muller, 1997 (note 1), ch 9), and more generally in US neo-conservative thought (Bell, 1996 (note 19)), but has also been a theme in the UK for the Social Affairs Unit in Britain and writers such as John O' Sullivan (O'Sullivan J, 1996, 'Conservatism and cultural identity' in Minogue, 1996 (note 2), 23-43).

33. Sennett R, 1980, *Authority*, Faber and Faber, London, 155; Tilly C, 1992, *Coercion, capital and European states, AD 990-1992*, Blackwell, Oxford.

34. Roger Scruton (1998, personal communication) suggests a settlement between neo-conservative and Oakeshottian ideas, whereby the state is not without purposes, but not defined by them. The problem is that even this goes beyond Oakeshott's strictures on the state as civil association. I take it that in the following oft-quoted passage, Oakeshott means exactly what he says, that the state is literally purposeless:

'In political activity, then, men sail a boundless and bottomless sea; there is neither harbour for shelter nor floor for anchorage; neither staring place nor appointed destination. The enterprise is to keep afloat on an even keel: the sea is both friend and enemy; and the seamanship consists in using resources of a traditional manner of behaviour to make a friend of every hostile occasion.' (Oakeshott M, 1956 [1951], 'Political education', in Laslett P, ed, *Philosophy, politics and society*, first series, Blackwell, Oxford, 1-21)

Oakeshott's 1956 edition footnote to this passage denying the relevance of the analogy between a journey and political commitment. 'Of course, the politician ... may before himself immediate tasks to be achieved; but this does not make the activity of politics itself a teleological activity.' I take him to mean that there are tasks necessary to keeping on an even keel, but no political tasks akin to setting a course for a destination.

The argument that I am making in the text is that no state that operated in this way could possibly legitimate itself. Modern publics expect much more, and more specific goals, and their expectations and demands have been measured over the decades since Oakeshott wrote those words, and found to be at once fundamental, relentless and consistent.

35. Douglas M, 1986, *How institutions think*, Routledge, London.

36. Douglas, 1986 (note 35).

37. The archetypical statement of that outlook is perhaps De Maistre. See Berlin I, 1990, 'Joseph de Maistre and the origins of fascism', in Berlin I, 1990, *The crooked timber of humanity: chapters in the history of ideas*, HarperCollins, London, 91-174. Mainstream liberal thought would regard the reactionary concept as one of power, not legitimate authority (see Wrong, 1996 (note 31), ch 2)

38. Sennett, 1980 (note 33), 166.

39. In particular, the 'Letters on a regicide peace' display a much coarser and more brutal sensibility than that displayed in the 'Reflections'. The author of the impeachment of Hastings or of the speeches on conciliation with the American colonies was concerned to combat exactly the kind of arbitrary power and military force that the author of the 'Letters on a regicide peace' calls to brought down upon corrupted France.

40. Used today by Simon Jenkins: see Jenkins, 1995 (note 15).

41. 6 P and Randon A, 1995, *Liberty, charity and politics*, Dartmouth Publishing, Aldershot.

42. Represented ably in one side of David Willetts' writings: Willetts, 1992 (note 1); Willetts, 1995 (Note 5), reprinted with a new epilogue in Gray and Willetts, 1997 (note 5). However, locked within the neo-conservative mainstream, it is hard for thinkers like Willetts to make clear just how far the autonomy of the central state can be abridged or how far protection from the individualist forces of less rooted market practice can be extended. This is a critique central to John Gray's communitarian thought: Gray J, 1997, *Endgames*, Polity, Cambridge.

43. For example, the well-known passages in the Reflections: 'When ancient opinions and rules of life are taken away, the loss cannot possibly be estimated... It is one of the excellences of a method in which time is amongst the assistants, that its operation is slow, and in some cases almost imperceptible... I would not exclude alteration either, but even when I changed, it should be to preserve'. For a twentieth century statement of the paleo-Burkean conservative preference for old institutions, see Oakeshott M, 'On being conservative', in Oakeshott, 1960 (note 12), reprinted in Kirk R, ed, 1982, *The portable conservative reader*, Penguin, New York, 567-599.

44. In a well-known passage in the 'Reflections', Burke remarks 'the state ought not to be considered nothing better than a partnership agreement in the trade of pepper and coffee, calico or tobacco, or some other such low concern, to be taken up for a little temporary interest, and to be dissolved at the fancy of the parties. It is to be looked on with other reverence;

because it is not a partnership in things subservient only to the gross animal existence of a temporary and perishable nature... it is a partnership not only between those who are living, but between those who are living, those who are dead, and those who are to be born.' Today, however, for all the inter-generational talk associated with some parts of the welfare state or the environmental movement's claims upon the state, loyalty and legitimacy depend crucially on what is offered and what is compensated between public authorities and current citizens, just as much as between forms of authority outside the central state and citizens.

6 P, 1998, 'New social contracts for the second modern age', paper presented at the conference, *Millennium Days: Setting off into the second modern age*, Kassel, Germany, 5 October 1998.
45. This is not to suggest that neo-Burkeans – or, for that matter, anyone else – ought to accept the general form of the precautionary principle. The precautionary principle, usually associated with radical environmentalism, states that, in advance of knowing the scale of the harms one wishes to prevent or the efficacy or the side-effects of the technology available to prevent them, one should make the over-cautious assumption that the risks will be unacceptably large and one should use any available technology that purposes to prevent them (O'Riordan T and Camerson J, eds, 1994, *Interpreting the precautionary principle*, Earthscan, London). The excesses that precautionary principle represents have sometimes been used to discredit any stance toward risk

other than the gung-ho.
46. Dodd P, 1995, *The battle over Britain*, Demos, London.
47. Birch D and McAvoy N, 1996, 'Downloadsamoney', *The new enterprise culture*, Demos Quarterly 8, Demos, London; Birch D, 1998, 'European multiple currencies: the e-euro and monetary union', *EuroVisions*, Demos Collection 13, Demos, London, 23-24.
48. Barnes J, 1998, *A federal Britain – no longer unthinkable*, Centre for Policy Studies, London.
49. Jenkins, 1995 (note 15).
50. Hayek, F von, 1979-1983, *Law, legislation and liberty: a new statement of the liberal principles of justice and political economy*, Routledge and Kegan Paul, London; Buchanan JM, 1975, *The limits of liberty: between anarchy and leviathan*, University of Chicago Press, Chicago; Buchanan JM, 1985, *Liberty, market and state: political economy in the 1980s*, New York University Press, New York; Buchanan JM, 1997, 'Can democracy promote the general welfare?', in Paul EF, Miller Jnr, FD, and Paul J, eds, 1997, *The welfare state*, Cambridge University Press, Cambridge, 165-179.
51. Tarling R and Dowds L, 1997, 'Crime and punishment' in Jowell R, Curtice J, Park A, Brook L, Thompson K and Bryson C, 1997, *British social attitudes: the fourteenth report: the end of Conservative values?*, Ashgate Press and SCPR, London.
52. Freedland J, 1998, *Bring home the revolution: how Britain can live the American dream*, Fourth Estate, London.
53. Boswell J and Peters J. 1997, *Capitalism in contention: business leaders and political economy in modern Britain*, Cambridge University Press, Cambridge.

54. Brittan S, 1996, *Capitalism with a human face*, Pan, London.
55. Oakeshott, 1960 (note 12).
56. Hayek F von, 1973-1982 (note 50) argued for a neo-liberalism that was optimistic without being rationalistic in the sense that Oakeshott and the neo-Burkeans would disapprove.
57. Mount, 1992 (note 14); Jenkins, 1995 (note 15).
58. Ideologies as diverse as Nazism, communitarianism and many of the varieties of feminism have not developed or offered a model of political economy, but have had clear political visions. However, the reverse is not the case: every model of political economy, however apparently technocratic its algebraic and graphical modelling, secretes ideology within itself. Models of political economy are, as I use the term, a subset of ideologies.